STEP-BY-STEP

Dried Flowers

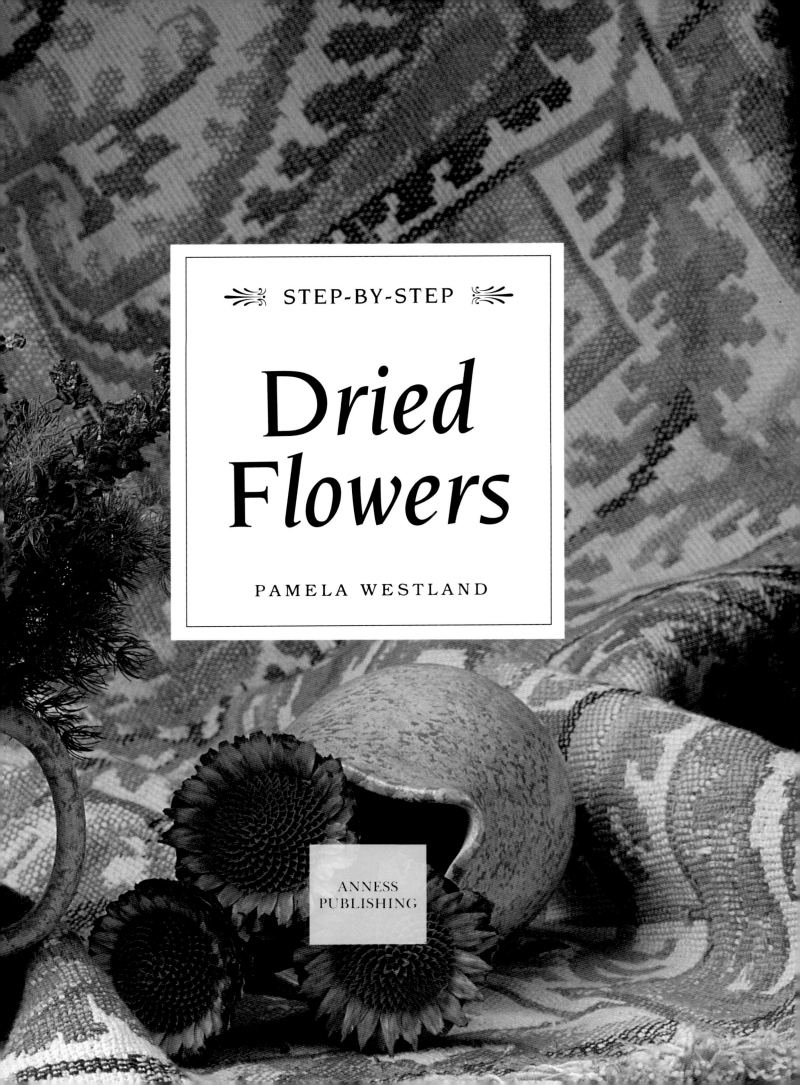

STEP-BY-STEP

Dried Flowers

PAMELA WESTLAND

ANNESS PUBLISHING

Produced by Anness Publishing Limited
1 Boundary Row
London SE1 8HP

Editorial Director: Joanna Lorenz
Series Editors: Judith Simons, Lindsay Porter
Photographer: Nelson Hargreaves
Designer: Tony Paine

Printed in Singapore by Star Standard Industries Pte. Ltd.

CONTENTS

INTRODUCTION

Preserving flowers, foliage, seedheads, and bracts is a delightfully simple yet infinitely satisfying pastime, and one which enables you to accumulate a collection of colourful and contrasting plant materials throughout the year. You can preserve materials from the garden or the countryside, dry flowers from a romantic gift or a wedding bouquet, or buy them from the ever-increasing variety available from florists.

We explain the preserving techniques in detail and then, in a series of step-by-step arrangements, show you how to enjoy your everlasting harvest in designs to decorate every room in the home and enhance every occasion.

A shallow bowl of paper-dry roses and carnations glowing in the candlelight; a profusion of flowers from all seasons classically arranged in a gilded urn; a pretty bridal bouquet of purple orchids and cream strawflowers that will become a treasured memento; a bowl lined with fragrant potpourri and luxuriant with flowers dried from the garden; a highly textured ring of pressed autumn leaves in deep, rich browns; and a charming gift basket composed of realistic fabric flowers: the art of decorating with preserved and man-made plant materials can transform every room in the house. With flowers, leaves, seedheads, and bracts that you have preserved yourself or bought from a shop, you can compose colourful and contrasting arrangements to give pleasure for months to come.

Colour, texture, and the infinite variety of combinations are the exciting keynotes of preserved materials. Brilliant pink peonies from a summer border; delphinium spires in deepest blue; statice and strawflowers in colours spanning the rainbow; bright scarlet iris seedpods, muted poppy and rue pods and old man's beard, offering woody and feathery textures. Using the variety of materials available, your designs can be as vibrant and colourful or as subtle and restrained as you like.

Collecting and preserving plant materials is a fulfilling and fascinating pastime you can enjoy throughout the year. If you have access to a garden, you can gather a few flowers from the borders as each season comes around, and preserve them using the simple methods described in the following pages. In summer you can cut branches of deciduous leaves and, later, bracts and berries to preserve, supple and glowing bright, in a solution of glycerin. As autumn approaches, you can cut seedheads and hang them to dry, or even dye them in natural-looking or more adventurous shades.

A walk in the woods becomes a treasure hunt for cones, interesting twigs, fallen leaves, pieces of gnarled wood, nuts, and acorns. A country walk may yield by the roadside a patch of wild oats, scattered wheat, interesting grasses, and other seedheads, partly dried on the plants and requiring only a few days in a warm, dry atmosphere to become practically everlasting. Even a walk on the beach will provide material. Pieces of sea-bleached driftwood make wonderful backdrops for dried-flower designs. Shells, if large enough, make luxurious-looking containers for dried flowers, and add a welcome sparkle to the design; and if small, they make light-catching and reflective accessories to a floral group. Coloured pebbles are a natural and attractive stem-holding material, while windswept stems of sea lavender, reeds, and rushes are all useful, versatile, and neutral filler materials.

A colourful container fitted with crumpled wire mesh netting holds the key to an arrangement of scarlet and orange berries – iris and pyracantha (firethorn) respectively – dried grasses and exotic seedheads. Many of these, bought without stems, are mounted on stub wires which are concealed among the surrounding materials. **Left**

Dried plant materials from the garden and wayside mingle in a casual grouping designed for the kitchen or dining room. The rugged basket is woven from bleached willow. **Opposite**

Florists' shops, department stores, boutiques, and even antique shops have a vast range of dried and preserved flowers and leaves for sale. Ceilings hanging with a floral arbour of dried flowers; buckets of preserved leaves; baskets and packets of exotic seedheads, many imported and perhaps unfamiliar – retail shops offer such variety and temptation, and are a useful source of materials for a growing collection. You could buy a bunch of rich pink dried rosebuds and dark blue larkspur and, with a few clippings of dried foliage and bracts, create a pretty countrified arrangement in an old teapot. The design illustrated below had matching afore-thought. The teapot and jug, both flea market bargains, are spatter-painted in pink and blue, the tiny speckled pattern a perfect foil for the contrasting round and spire shapes.

You could buy an assortment of dried seedheads, some like ornately carved ornaments, and mount them on stub-wire stems (many are sold stemless), then blend them with reds and greens from your collection. There might be lotus flower seedheads, trumpet-shaped and peppered with holes; luffa (loofah) seedpods with their chestnut-brown colouring and high-ridged texture; protea flowers, a striking combination of wood-brown and silver sold at various stages of development; jhuta pods like wide-open sculpted flowers; and plumosum heads with their wayward spiky appearance. Take any two or three of these plant types, arrange them with feathery and frondy materials – the very antithesis of their harsh outlines – and you have created a plant sculpture. The 'Eastern Riches' project in which the materials are arranged in a yogurt pot – you could equally use a wide-necked jug – shows only one of the effects that can be achieved.

HARVESTING PLANT MATERIALS

It can be immensely satisfying to gather plant materials from a garden or in the wild, knowing that by preserving them you can prolong or even enhance their decorative life. Many flowers and some leaves can be preserved by air-drying – often no more than being hung in bunches in a warm, airy room – and a wide range of others can be dried in a desiccant. Leaves gathered when the sap is still rising in the plant, as well as some bracts, can be preserved, glowing and supple, in a solution of water and glycerin, and may take on shades and tints more attractive even than those of autumn.

Before launching into the countryside with a pair of secateurs or pruning shears, take note that stringent restrictions apply to the cutting of wild plants. These limitations vary from country to country and state to state, according to the local abundance or scarcity of plant types; what is a rampant weed in one area may be a protected species in another. Be sure you know the rules before cutting even one stem.

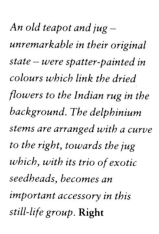

An old teapot and jug – unremarkable in their original state – were spatter-painted in colours which link the dried flowers to the Indian rug in the background. The delphinium stems are arranged with a curve to the right, towards the jug which, with its trio of exotic seedheads, becomes an important accessory in this still-life group. **Right**

Gather these materials – lavender, rosebuds, wheat, and grasses – at the height of summer, dry them in a warm, dry atmosphere, and enjoy the fragrant arrangement for months to come. **Left**

A dried-flower tree makes an attractive table or windowsill decoration that is both easy to make and long lasting. This one, composed on a dry foam sphere on a knobbly twig, is studded with white statice, lavender, and a variety of seedheads. **Below**

FLOWERS

Plant material for drying should, ideally, be harvested when it is completely free of extraneous moisture. If you have to gather flowers when they are wet, toss them gently on blotting paper to remove surface water, and stand the stems in a container of water in a warm, dry room until the petals are thoroughly dry. Do not be tempted to start one of the drying processes while the flowers are still damp. The development of mould will rapidly gain ground on the drying technique – a recipe for disappointment.

The time of day is also a contributory factor to successful drying. It is best to gather the flowers for drying before or after the sun is at its highest; it does not matter about seedheads. At high noon the plant is at its most vulnerable, and more inclined to wilt than respond to the drying treatment.

Flowers to be dried by one of the free-circulation-of-air techniques include many of those which may be described as multi-floral stems – clarkia, delphinium, heather, larkspur, and mimosa, among others – and those composed of a mass of florets – achillea (yarrow), golden-rod, and lady's mantle are examples. Flowers of this type are best harvested at the mid-way stage of their development. In the case of delphinium, this means when some of the lowest florets are fully opened, the ones above them are just beginning to unfurl, and the top-most buds are still tightly closed.

Other flowers that dry successfully in warm air are those composed of a mass of petals, such as cornflowers, love-in-a-mist, and pot marigolds. These should be harvested just before they are fully opened. All everlastings, including statice and strawflowers, are also well suited to

The gourds placed beside the dried flower and seed arrangement, echoing the raised pattern on the jug, are seen as complementary accessories. The flowers and seedheads, in a low colour key, include lady's mantle, strawflowers, statice, linseed (flaxseed), wheat, and bells of Ireland. **Left**

A glorious array of dried flowers forms the prettiest of veils for a north-facing bedroom window. The blue and white jug is fitted with crumpled wire mesh netting to secure the profusion of delphinium, rosebuds, sea lavender, and strawflowers. **Opposite**

this drying technique. If the weather is favourable, these flowers may be left on the plant until they are crackle-dry, but in unsettled conditions, when storms or strong gales are forecast, it is best to gather them on a dry day and hang them in bunches indoors to complete the drying process that is part of their natural cycle.

Desiccant drying opens up opportunities to preserve jewel-bright anemones, golden narcissus, and fragrant stems of lily-of-the-valley, as well as camellias, orchids, roses, and many other species. These may be harvested at any stage of their cycle, from tiny bud to full-blown bloom. In terms of design versatility, it can be rewarding to gather a few flowers at a time, and preserve them at the various stages of their development. In that way, you can capture the natural progression of each flower, and enjoy the variety of shape and colour in arrangements that will be a reminder of a continuing harvest.

Alternatively, you can cut flowers at an early stage and arrange them, fresh, just the way they are. Then, when they are just at their peak, you can preserve them in desiccant. This approach allows you to enjoy the beauty of fresh flowers before you preserve them, which is particularly welcome when you have been given a special token of flowers. Keep a watchful eye on them and preserve the flowers for all time.

SEEDHEADS

Harvesting seedheads for drying offers further rich pickings in terms of shape and texture, as many of the photographs here show. You might like to arrange a cluster of poppy seedheads in a winter garden composition in a basket, their clearly defined, urn-like shapes making a dramatic silhouette. You might choose to arrange a handful of linseed (flaxseed) heads, the tiny ball-like

The air-drying process has long-term decorative potential. Hanging in bunches and standing upright in containers, the flowers and seedheads can decorate the corner of a room, or compose a still-life group.
Right

shapes an attractive foil to spiky ears of wheat and petal-packed peonies in a design with more than a hint of the 1930s. Or in a different mood, you might decide to combine fluffy heads of hare's-tail grass, wheat ears, lavender seedheads, and silvery honesty 'moons' with dried ruby-red roses as a romantic decoration for a heart-shaped vine wreath form.

Seedhead gathering is a less exacting science than harvesting flowers, though it is desirable to leave the seed carriers on wild plants until the seeds have scattered and the following year's crop is assured. Moisture is the only threat, so gather the stems when they are dry, or, if this is not possible, toss them on absorbent paper and hang or stand them loosely in bunches in a dry place. Do not allow damp seedheads to jostle together. When air cannot circulate freely between plant materials trouble occurs in the form of bacterial growth.

FOLIAGE

Preserved leaves are an invaluable component in dried-flower compositions of all kinds. Long foliage sprays such as eucalyptus can be used to 'sketch in' the outline of arrangements before the flowers are positioned, and small sprays of dried leaves arranged among dried rosebuds and carnations separate the flowers, allowing each to be seen in clear outline. Foliage is also ideal for concealing the holding materials of a design. It is well worthwhile building up a collection of preserved leaves to supplement and complement your dried flowers and seedheads.

A few types of foliage can be preserved by the air-drying method, including sage, santolina, lavender, lady's mantle, and hops. Many more can be dried in a desiccant, and both evergreens and deciduous leaves can be preserved in glycerin. For the most satisfactory results, it is best to gather deciduous leaves once they have fully matured on the tree or shrub, and while the sap is still rising. Beautiful as they are in their soft-green immaturity, young leaves do not take well to the preserving processes,

and will wilt under the strain. Evergreens have a longer harvest potential, but even those should not be cut when they are showing young green shoots.

AIR-DRYING PLANT MATERIALS

The simplest and most widely used method of preserving plant materials is by air-drying, which may mean no more than leaving them in a suitable room where warm, dry air can circulate freely around them. This process is not an exact science and the actual temperature is not critical, though it should not fall below 10°C (50°F.) More important is the humidity: a damp, steamy atmosphere where the windows are streaming with condensation is definitely not one in which to dry flowers. In conditions like this, the materials will absorb moisture more quickly than they shed it. This rules out, as the drying room, some kitchens, bathrooms, and utility rooms, and many garden sheds or garages. However, living rooms and bedrooms can be used successfully, and bunches of flowers hanging from the ceiling, on a pole across a room corner, on an airing rack, or on coathangers on a wall can be a positive decorative feature.

Some plant types, mostly those with a heavy head-to-stem ratio, give the best results when dried upright, the stems loosely held in tall containers and the heads fanning out wide and away from each other to ensure the free circulation of air. Materials in this category include umbrella-shaped flowers and seedheads, also known as umbellifers, such as achillea (yarrow), fennel, caraway, and onion seedheads; others in that family include pampas grass, globe artichokes, linseed (flaxseed), and corn cobs (Indian corn).

Other flowers and foliage may be dried horizontally, spread out on racks or shelves covered with absorbent paper. Dock and sorrel seedheads, grasses, and lavender are among the plant types that respond well to this method, but they will do so only if they are first arranged in a single layer and then turned at frequent intervals. Change the paper if it becomes the slightest bit damp.

Some plant materials may be air-dried, though it seems a contradiction in terms, with their stems standing in a little water, no more than 4–5 cm (1½–2in). The principle is that as the stems gradually absorb the water it evaporates and eventually, over a week or ten days, the plant material dries more or less naturally. Flowers and bracts in this category include cornflowers, mimosa, gypsophila, pearl (pearly) everlasting, and hydrangea.

Many plant types can be dried by more than one method. It is often a matter of choice and convenience whether you hang flowers and seedheads in bunches, stand them in a container, or spread them out flat. To repeat, drying is not an exact science, and there is plenty of scope for choice and experimentation.

Whatever drying method you choose, the choice and preparation of plant materials is of paramount importance. It is simply not worth preserving bird-damaged sprays of foliage or flowers that are even slightly discoloured. Snip off any unsightly leaves – the largest ones of purple sage, for example, are prone to turn brittle and brown around the edges, and will never revive – and pull off any off-colour flower petals. It is often possible to rescue flowers, especially roses, which show only minimal damage to their petals.

In a few cases, leaves will air-dry almost as satisfactorily as the flowers on the same stems; roses are a good example. In others, the leaves become brittle and snap off, so it is best to remove them at the preparation stage. Chinese lanterns (winter cherry) are a case in point. While the seedpods, changing from pale green to brilliant orange, dry to perfection, the leaves fall to the ground. Strip off any leaves and florets that would be squashed and trapped under the string when they are tied in bunches. If the air cannot reach all of the plant material rot sets in and impairs the drying process.

Materials to be dried by hanging should be tied into small bunches, with large stems tied individually. Arrange candidates for upright or horizontal drying accordingly, and leave the materials in a warm, dry place for several days. After that, check every two or three days. When dry enough – when they feel crisp and papery – remove them from the extra warmth of an airing cupboard or boiler cupboard and store them at ordinary room temperature, but still in a dry atmosphere. You can store materials as you please and as you dry them. They make an attractive feature hanging in bunches or standing in containers, or they can be packed carefully in boxes until needed.

DRYING IN WATER

Hydrangea heads and gypsophila, so different in size, shape, and form, are two of the plant materials which can be air-dried with their stems standing in a little water.

Give a hearth-side decoration an airing when having drinks or tea on the patio. The design includes peonies and rosebuds, sea lavender and strawflowers, marjoram and carthamus. **Opposite**

If a kitchen is well ventilated, then air-drying or dried herbs and flowers hanging in bunches can be a homely and attractive feature. They are also conveniently on hand when needed for cooking or garnishing. **Right**

DRYING IN DESICCANTS

When that time comes, you may have enough air-dried materials to compose a towering arrangement to stand in the hearth. There could be acanthus and achillea (yarrow) flowers, goldenrod and globe amaranth, tansy and timothy grass. On a smaller scale, you could bind dried flowers into a posy and hang on a chair back or bedpost: pretty, creamy-white feverfew combined with strawflowers and rosebuds, lady's mantle and lavender, all tied with trailing ribbons.

But as far as drying is concerned, this represents little more than the tip of the iceberg. By adding the technique of drying in desiccants you can extend your collection to include trumpet- and cone-shaped flowers, such as daffodils and freesia; composites like spray chrysanthemums, marguerites, and other daisy forms; open-faced flowers, such as pansies, anemones, and buttercups; high-density flowers like ranunculus, carnations, and many more.

If air-drying is seen as an almost natural technique, in which air alone draws out the plant moisture, then desiccant-drying may be thought of as the scientific approach. In this method, any one of a number of drying agents may be used to fill every cavity and crevice of the plant material, cover every part of every surface and, in so doing, support the flower and keep it perfectly in shape. That is why hollow and flat forms, which would collapse or wilt during the air-drying process, emerge from the desiccant having lost none of their original characteristics, and looking as fresh as ever. The 'Candle Glow' arrangement uses flowers dried in this way.

Your choice of desiccant may depend on the quantity and scale of the plant materials you intend to dry. But be warned: once you have experienced the thrill of gently scraping away the crystals or powder to discover the perfectly dried forms of, say, trumpet-shaped mallow flowers, purple-spotted foxgloves, and fully-opened roses you may never want to stop!

TYPES OF DESICCANT

The desiccant options available are alum powder (aluminum sulfate) and household borax, both of which may be bought in chemists (drugstores) and are suitable for small, delicate flower types; ground silica gel crystals, available in some chemists, florists' shops and camera retailers, and suitable for all the small-to-medium-sized flowers and above; corn meal, from grocers and supermarkets, for flowers of all sizes; and dry silver sand, recommended for drying large quantities of sizeable materials, such as dahlias and mophead chrysanthemums.

Silica gel crystals are available in two forms – standard white crystals, which look like colourless coffee sugar, and the colour-changing type that have a built-in moisture indicator. These crystals are bright blue when they are dry and ready to use, and turn white and then pink when they are damp. If bought in large crystal form silica gel is too heavy to be used successfully for drying flowers, and you have to grind it into fine crystals – not quite to a powder –

using a pestle and mortar, or an electric blender or food processor. If you do use an electric appliance, take it to an open window before removing the lid. A swirl of very fine dust, which looks like thick fog, will rush upwards as you do so. It can cause irritation to the throat and eyes, so keep the appliance well away from your face.

You may like to experiment by using a combination of two or more of the desiccants. Adding, say, one part silica gel crystals or dry silver sand to two or three parts alum or borax helps to overcome a problem commonly experienced when either of the powders is used alone: they both have tenacious sticking properties, and can be difficult to brush off dry and brittle petals. You may also like to weigh up the relative costs, though over the long term the difference becomes almost negligible since all the desic-

A heart-shaped vine wreath form decorated with dried flowers would make a delightfully romantic Valentine or birthday gift. The posies of roses, sea lavender, honesty, *wheat, lamb's-ear grasses, and gypsophila are bound to a central core of twisted stub wires and the design is finished with a paper ribbon bow.*
Above

cants can be sieved to remove any scraps of petals or leaves that may have been displaced, spread on baking trays, and dried in an oven at low temperature. Put in the oven a tray of bright pink silica gel crystals that have drawn out the moisture from a box of carnations, leave it for half an hour or so, and retrieve sky-blue crystals ready for use. Allow the desiccants to cool, then store them in an airtight tin or jar. In this way, desiccants can be used almost indefinitely. Some flower-arranging enthusiasts of our acquaintance have just celebrated the 20th anniversary of a tin full of silica gel!

METHODS

The method is simple. Spread a thin layer of desiccant in a container, arrange the flowers and foliage sprays according to type, well spaced and with no two items touching, and cover them gently, gradually, and completely with desiccant until it forms a top layer about 1.5cm (½in) above the plant material.

The type of container you use depends on the speed of the drying method you choose. The traditional, slow way

is to put the plant materials and any of the desiccants in an airtight tin, close the lid, and set it aside for two, three, or more days, depending on the density and moisture content of the materials to be dried. Very carefully brush or scrape away the desiccant when you think the time is right, and very gently brush it over the plant materials again if you find they are not paper-crisp.

You can speed up the process by drying the plant materials in a desiccant in an oven at the lowest temperature. Layer them in an ovenproof dish of any kind (you needn't use a lid), and process them with the door slightly ajar. If you use silica gel crystals alone, a dish of, say, six peonies should be dry in 20–25 minutes; a mixture of silica gel and any of the other drying agents increases the time factor by about 50%. Check the progress every two or three minutes once you think they should be ready. Over-processing makes the materials unacceptably brittle.

The fastest means of drying plant materials in a desiccant is in a microwave. Layer them in a microwave-proof container – anything (without a lid) from an earthenware or toughened glass dish to a cardboard box – and process on low power. Drying times vary according to the properties of the appliance, the type of container used, and the density and moisture-content of the plants; it is best to experiment, check on progress every minute or so, and make notes of the processing times.

DESICCANT DRYING

1 Fully-opened roses on very short stems and a spray of Singapore orchids are arranged on a layer of silica gel crystals in a microwave-safe dish.

2 The silica gel crystals, which are blue before processing, are sprinkled carefully around and over the flowers. When they are fully covered with the desiccant they can be dried in an oven or a microwave.

As a general guide, a shoe box of six carnations in silica gel crystals dried in the test microwave in seven minutes; four short sprays of delphinium, plus two extra florets, in seven minutes; and four rosebuds, in five minutes. Four short but thick sprays of elaeagnus (silver berry) leaves, also in silica gel, took four minutes to dry, and four short sprays of mimosa flowers and leaves – pretty as fillers in dried arrangements – took four and a half minutes. You may find it preferable to process the materials for a slightly shorter 'cooking' time, and then leave them to dry – but only for five to ten minutes – in the desiccant.

There are good reasons – apart from the sheer joy of being able to unearth perfect dried-flower forms every few minutes – for using one of the above heating methods with desiccants. Since the speeded-up processes utilize the drying agents for a much shorter time, you can quickly preserve a batch of flowers that all come to the peak of perfection at the same time; process wildflowers and

leaves the day you gather them; and dry a treasured composition, a child bridesmaid's headdress for example, before the flowers have time to fade. In such a case, once the flowers are dry you can reassemble them on the circlet or band to keep as a decorative memento.

PREPARATION OF PLANT MATERIAL

Whichever desiccant drying method you choose, you must prepare the flowers and foliage in a similar way. Flower stalks do not respond well to the treatment, and in any case they take up too much space. Imagine the depth of silica gel crystals you would need to dry a fully-opened rose standing upright on a 15cm (6in) stem! Cut individual flowers such as roses, peonies, and pansies to leave short stalks, no more than 1.5cm (½in). Cut flowers with thick calyces, such as carnations and daffodils, just below the calyx, and cut flower sprays like lily-of-the-valley and grape hyacinth (*Muscari*) to leave about 2.5cm (1in) of stalk. If you are using the room temperature or the conventional oven method of desiccant drying, you can, at this stage, push short lengths of stub wire into short, fleshy stems; it makes it easier to wire them onto false stems later. *Please note: you must not use wire of any kind if the materials are to be processed in a microwave.*

Once you have spread a layer of desiccant in the container, position separate flowers upright, so they can be filled most easily with the drying agent, and flower and leaf sprays on their sides. Supporting each upright flower in turn with one hand, spoon the desiccant under it until it takes the shape of the flower; care at this stage makes the difference between average and perfect results. Then sprinkle the desiccant gently, not in a heavy onslaught, over the flower until it is covered. Sprinkle on a covering layer, and process by your preferred method.

A dried-flower panel makes a pleasing impact, whether decorating an exterior wall for a garden party, the back of an unused fireplace, a wall niche, or an arch. The base is made of a double thickness of wire mesh netting enclosing sphagnum moss, and the flowers and seedheads are wired into bunches and hooked into the mesh. **Left**

Restrained use of colour in a floral ring puts the accent on texture. This design, which would be suitable as a desk or table top decoration, includes sage and purple sage, hydrangea and marjoram, and deep red roses and sea lavender arranged on a dry foam ring. **Opposite**

Microwave-drying makes possible a glorious profusion of flowers from all seasons. This creamware mug holds a medley of flowers surrounded by dried foliage sprays. There are roses in various stages of development, carnations and spray carnations, Singapore orchids and freesias, larkspur and mimosa, spray chrysanthemums and daffodils – dried flowers that have to be touched to be believed. **Below**

As you gently brush the desiccant after processing, you should find that the flowers with a strong, deep colour, such as purple Singapore orchids, ruby-red carnations, and dark blue delphinium, have held their colour perfectly. Middle-toned flowers may have faded a little, and some white and pale cream examples, from arum lilies to marguerites, freesias, and primroses, may have turned the delicate colour of parchment. Not all white flowers respond in that way, and some – daisies, dogwood, and candytuft, for example – have been known to emerge dazzling white.

Just how true to colour and how dazzlingly white the materials seem to be at this stage will depend on the type of desiccant used, but they all adhere to the petals and leaves to a greater or lesser extent, covering them with a dusty film. Carefully lift out the preserved materials, which by now will be very brittle, and shake them to remove loose desiccant. Then, using a small camel-hair or similar type of paintbrush, gently brush all the plant surfaces. It can be an exciting revelation when what seemed like a misty grey rose emerges as a wine-red beauty, or what looked like a spray of silver-grey leaves appears with the original green and yellow speckles.

Most plant materials dried in this way, having little or no natural stem, will need to be mounted on false wire stems before being arranged. Details of the various wiring techniques are given later in this book. You can use the flowers in other forms of flowercraft too, attaching them, for example, to a stem ring base to make a floral circlet.

MICROWAVE-DRYING

Open-drying in a microwave is a relatively new technique that can be applied to a range of materials. It is particularly suitable for plants such as gypsophila, lady's mantle, marjoram, tansy, goldenrod, and sedum (stonecrop), which are composed of a mass of florets, and others such as cornflower and feverfew, which are made of a mass of petals. As the flowers dry, the loss of volume and shape is barely discernible. Foliage that dries well by this method includes fennel, sage and purple sage, and silver-leaved types such as santolina, senecio (ground sel), and lavender. This is also a fail-safe way to dry hydrangeas.

Cut the material into sprays of suitable lengths; there is no need to cut off flower stems. Cover the microwave turntable or a suitable plate with a double thickness of kitchen paper towels, and arrange the plant materials in a single layer, no two items touching. To dry cornflowers, for example, you can arrange them in a wheel pattern, heads facing outwards, stems to the middle. Dry the materials on low power for as long as it takes.

In the test microwave, a whole hydrangea head took seven minutes, and retained its pale blue colouring perfectly; a whole head of sedum took six minutes and this, too, kept its colour well; about 12 cornflowers took five minutes and dried very successfully while a plate of short sprays of goldenrod took three minutes.

PRESERVING IN GLYCERIN

Preserving foliage, bracts, and berries in a glycerin and water solution adds a further dimension to a collection of long-lasting plant materials. Branches and small sprays of deciduous evergreen leaves blend well in arrangements with dried flowers and, with their high-gloss appearance, provide an interesting texture contrast. Bracts such as

Arrange dried flowers in natural profusion, and create a design with the appeal of a cottage garden. The materials *include marjoram, love-in-a-mist seedheads, achillea (yarrow), rosebuds, and strawflowers.* **Above**

bells of Ireland have an almost architectural quality, and preserved berries from glossy red rosehips to dense black blackberries retain the warm aura of autumn fruits.

In the preserving process, the glycerin solution is taken up by the stems and carried to every part of the plant material, to the very tip of every leaf. As the water evaporates, the plant cells retain the glycerin, and are held in a decorative state of suspended animation.

Most materials undergo some colour change in the process. Beech leaves, one of the most attractive examples of preserved foliage, turn dark chestnut brown, eucalyptus deepens to a dark gun-metal blue, and laurel leaves become almost black. Bay and rosemary darken only slightly and – an added bonus – retain their scent, while acanthus leaves darken considerably. Most berries shrink a little in the process, a transition barely noticeable in a cluster, and some deepen in tone. Yellow holly berries, for example, turn bright orange, and some red berries mellow to a shade of burnt umber.

If you gather materials throughout the year you can practise a conveyor-belt system of preserving, reusing, and topping up the solution for each successive batch.

To prepare woody stems, scrape the bark about 5cm (2in) from the ends, and split or crush the stem ends so they can most easily take up the preserving liquid. Discard damaged leaves or bracts, and any lower ones that would be trapped in the container.

Make up a solution of one part glycerin, which you can buy from chemists and drugstores, and two parts very hot water. Mix it thoroughly, and pour it into a heatproof container to a depth of about 5cm (2in). Stand the stems in the solution, making sure the ends are submerged. An alternative method, which gives better results with large, fleshy leaves such as acanthus, Japanese fatsia, aspidistra (cast-iron plant), fig, and hosta (plantain lily), is to completely immerse them in a 'bath' of the solution, in a shallow container.

The process time varies according to the size and density of the materials, and it may take anything from three or four days to two or three weeks. When the material is fully preserved, it should be supple, with no traces of brittleness, and have changed colour evenly throughout; it may also show beads of moisture on the surface. If during the process the tips of some leaves start

GLYCERIN PRESERVING

1 Preserving foliage and berries in a glycerin and hot water solution brings them into the almost everlasting category.

2 Large fleshy leaves such as acanthus (shown here), Japanese fatsia, hosta (plantain lily), fig, and some types of ivy are best preserved flat, in a shallow dish, covered with the glycerin and hot water solution.

A rectangular basket is painted purple to match the marjoram that forms the foundation of the arrangement. Wheat and delphinium spires provide the 'points', and peonies, clusters of carthamus, and globe artichoke heads the 'rounds'. Silhouetted against the matt black of the stove, the arrangement makes a lively display all through the summer. **Below**

Dried-flower posies have a natural charm that may be lacking in some formal arrangements. They can hang on any vertical surface from a wall to a door, a bedpost to a chair back. This one is made up of cream rosebuds and lady's mantle with red miniature rosebuds and white sea lavender. **Right**

to dry – which can happen before the solution reaches them – rub the surface on both sides with cotton wool or a tissue soaked in the preservative. And if the plant material takes up the solution before it is fully preserved, top up the container with some more.

When the plant material is preserved, wipe large leaves with a dry cloth to remove any stickiness, and dry the stems thoroughly. Wash and dry leaves that have been immersed. Store the materials upright in dry containers, layered between papers in a box, or hanging in bunches in a cool room, away from strong light. Strain any leftover preserving solution and store it in an airtight bottle for future use.

ADDING TINTS

As stated above, the process of preserving plant materials in a glycerin solution almost invariably brings about a colour change. Some materials, especially leaves, may take on the nearly natural tints and shades of autumn, while others will emerge considerably darker. You may adapt the preserving process and cheat nature still further by adding a little water-soluble dye to the preserving solution, either to intensify natural-looking colours or achieve artificial ones.

Green dye is particularly effective with deciduous leaves such as beech, (but not copper beech), chestnut, oak, and maple, and with ivy and rhododendron, all of which emerge from the treatment with varying shades of deep, rich green and no hint of brown. Copper beech, maple, and eucalyptus leaves take well to a red or rust-coloured dye solution, which turns them copper-bronze, and bells of Ireland bracts and hydrangea flower heads present an opportunity to intensify their appeal with the addition of green, red, or blue colouring.

For a completely different approach and markedly different results, you can add a little bleach to the preserving solution – about one part in ten – to give leaves and bracts a light, bright, sun-drenched look. Sprays of preserved and bleached fern leaves, the colour of pale parchment, are especially pretty in summery arrangements of dried rosebuds and pansies.

Dye can also be added to the water used in one of the air-drying processes. As the plant materials take up the liquid, they also take up the dye, and change colour in the process. You can try the technique with hydrangeas to intensify or exaggerate their natural colour; with gypsophila, which looks especially attractive when dyed pale pink or blue; and with white pearl (pearly) everlasting and sea lavender, whose lack of natural colour gives you a clean palette on which to impose any colour.

Many seedheads are characterized by the modesty and subtlety of their colouring, which can be both attractive in its own right and a foil to more obviously showy dried materials. There may be a time however, when you feel that some seedheads in your collection would benefit from more colour. You can transform mallow stems, their seedpods like small fat stars; lupins (lupines) like silver-grey rabbits' ears; candytuft with whorls of seeds in clusters; dainty stems of grape hyacinths; flat discs of honesty, and many others by dip-dyeing or spraying.

This imposed colouring can never be an exact art, since the tones achieved will be influenced by the absorption properties of the various plants and the amount of residual moisture they have retained, but this makes the process all the more fascinating.

For traditional dip-dyeing, you can use a natural dye made from dyers' pokeweed or woad, or, more readily available, onion skins simmered in water to make a brown dye, or even marigold petals – one cup petals and one cup water simmered for an hour to achieve a pale yellow colour. For more vibrant shades and beautiful heathery tones, use the strained and cooled juice from stewed blackberries, mulberries, raspberries, red-currants, and gooseberries (which make a pale, amber-coloured dye). Commercial dyes can also be used. Pour the colorant into jars, or, to dye long stems, shallow trays or baking dishes, and dip in the dried plant materials for a few seconds. It is a mistake to leave them for a long soak; all seedheads are inclined to become soggy. Shake the dyed materials over several layers of newspaper and hang them to dry in a warm, airy room with newspapers underneath them.

After dyeing a few experimental stems, you will discover that the soft and fur-like texture of lupins (lupines) and ballota absorb the colour most readily and emerge with the deepest shades; that Jerusalem sage,

Dip-dyeing is a technique that can be used to give sun-bleached seedheads a new and colourful personality. Natural plant dyes and strained fruit juices, as here, can be used, or commercial dyes can be bought. The secret is to immerse the materials for only a few seconds, and retrieve them before they become soggy. **Above**

knapweed, grape hyacinth, poppy, and teasel are in the medium absorption range; and that honesty takes up the colour only grudgingly and looks as if it has been casually splashed with colour. The 'Colourful Personality' arrangement shows what a dramatic effect can be created with a blend of purple-dyed seedheads and the natural brilliance of Chinese lanterns (winter cherry).

For even more positive results, you can spray dried seedheads and preserved leaves with non-toxic florists' paints, which are available in practically any colour of your choice. If possible, work out of doors, or in a shed or garage. Cover the surface with newspaper, stand the stems upright in a container or hold them in your hand, and spray them all around with light, even strokes. Poppy seedheads can be painted bright scarlet, teasels sprayed a vibrant green, the centres of sunflowers and gaillardia coloured sunshine yellow, and leaves spatter-sprayed metallic gold or silver. The technique opens up new possibilities amounting to a second decorative harvest.

CONTAINERS AND EQUIPMENT

Think of any container you might consider filling to overflowing with fresh flowers, any vase or urn, jug or mug, bowl or basket, can or packet, and then think of some more. That's how varied the possibilities are for dried-flower holders. A container does not have to be waterproof and will not need a moisture-proof liner. It doesn't even have to be a vessel of any kind. You can tie a posy of dried flowers to a wooden spoon or a Polynesian hand brush to make a highly individual decoration for the kitchen; arrange wheat, lavender, strawflowers, and roses in a wire basket lined with moss; and bind dried-flower posies to a hatband for a millinery decoration that will never falter. You can arrange a bundle of Chinese lanterns (winter cherry), ranging from green to orange, in a bundle of bamboo poles, or create a swag of dried flowers, seedheads, cereals, and grasses on a wire frame. By using preformed dry foam shapes available at florists, you can create dried-flower trees with the neatness of topiary;

Spray painting can give dried or fresh plant materials a new and more colourful personality, or bring a sparkle to their appearance. Use non-toxic paints, and work out of doors or close to an open window to minimize the effect of the fumes. **Left**

A kitchen basket, more often used to hold eggs or bread rolls, makes a low-key container for dried flowers. It is lined with sphagnum moss and fitted with dry foam to hold a fan shape of lavender, preserved eucalyptus, wheat, and strawflowers. **Opposite**

Whenever dried flowers and foliage are arranged in stem-holding foam, it should be of the dry, non-absorbent type, which is usually grey or brown and has a sparkly finish. This type is more stable for dried-flower work than absorbent foam used dry (which is not recommended), but the two kinds do share one important feature: they are equally unattractive to look at. Therefore, similar arts of concealment are called for in dried-flower work: short-stemmed flowers recessed into a design and positioned close against the foam; clusters of leaves, or large individual ones, positioned at the base of an arrangement; and snippings – they may be of oats, lady's mantle, or hydrangea – pressed into camouflage service when the design is almost finished. To check there is no likelihood that a glint of foam is showing through, it is a good idea to turn a strong light onto a completed arrangement, or take it to a window, and check it from every angle.

Stems, too, can present another challenge in the matter of concealment. Dried stems, whether they support bunches of air-dried rosebuds or microwave-dried

or compose dried-flower rings, pretty circlets to give as a token for weddings, christenings, and anniversaries.

Most of the equipment, or mechanics, used for fresh-flower arrangements can be applied to dried-flower designs as well. You can fit a jug or vase with a piece cut from a block of stem-holding foam and hold it in place with narrow strips of florists' adhesive tape; press a cylinder of foam into a purpose-made plastic saucer, and secure it with florists' adhesive clay to the neck of a tall container, so that stems may be angled in any direction; and press a piece of foam onto the prongs of a plastic spike fixed to a wooden board or shallow dish. You can tape or wire a piece of foam to a woven placemat and arrange dried flowers for a wall decoration, or bind dried-flower posies with florists' silver wire and press them into a vine wreath form or other ring shape with staples cut from stub wires. Tape a piece of foam to the handle of a basket, and trail dried flowers and leaves to follow the curve, or use foam to secure a nosegay to the neck of a bottle.

cornflowers, may have lost some of their original colour and characteristics, but they are natural and will pass in a crowd. But false wire stems, even when wrapped in all-enveloping bands of gutta percha (floral) tape, can look unacceptably harsh and need to be kept out of sight.

To meet this requirement, you simply have to arrange the dried flowers and foliage in close proximity, the way they would appear in a well-stocked flower border. You could dry all the flowers and foliage sprays in desiccants in a microwave, and mount all the flowers, and many of the leaf sprays on stub wires.

To create a more open design, and still not reveal the secret of the false stems, you can arrange a foundation of foliage and flower sprays as in the 'Candle Glow' arrangement, and conceal the wire-mounted materials – the roses, carnations, and anemones – among them.

Another solution is to use dried natural stems such as wheat or rye as false stems for other dried materials. Simply push the short stem of a cluster of hydrangea florets or a strawflower into the hollow stalk to elevate the plant material to new and natural-looking heights. The 'Birthday Basket' arrangement shows how decorative and visually acceptable wheat stalks can be.

POSIES, SWAGS, AND WREATHS

A free-style bunch of papery flowers comprising a country-style wall or table decoration; a dried-flower posy adorning the bride's chair at a wedding; an elegant floral ribbon outlining the top table at a family celebration party; a hay-covered ring studded with the brightest and boldest dried flowers imaginable; a vine wreath form covered with scented lavender – preserved materials have a variety of roles to play in the composition of bunches, posies, swags, and wreaths.

On the spur of the moment, you can gather a handful of dried flowers into a sheaf or bunch that has a casual, unstudied charm. Place the longest stems flat on a work surface, cover them with dried flower heads in diminishing ranks, arrange a few wayward stems to give width and wispiness at the sides, bind the stems with twine, raffia or florists' silver wire, and finish the design with a raffia or ribbon bow. Hanging bunches such as this find a decorative place in the hallway, kitchen, living room, or bedroom according to the materials you choose. They can be designed, too, with an air of calculated informality, to grace the most formal of occasions, such as a wedding.

A posy or bouquet to be carried by a bride or her bridesmaids calls for more attention to detail, and in many cases the flowers will need to be wired. This technique not only serves the purpose of mounting short-stemmed dried materials onto false wire stems, but also lends flexibility to the design – you can bend wire stems in a manner not possible with natural ones – and minimizes the girth and clumsiness of the handle. The project for a bridal bouquet included here, a pretty cascade of dried and wired roses, orchids, statice, strawflowers, carnations, and hydrangea, is designed to become a romantic family heirloom in the Victorian tradition.

Floral ribbons and swags are in keeping with a much longer tradition, that of enhancing the setting for a special occasion – whether a wedding or a festival – with garlands of flowers. By using dried and preserved flowers and foliage you can compose a garland gradually, and well in advance of the occasion, adding to it whenever you have a few moments to spare. Best of all, dried-flower garlands will retain their good looks whatever the weather and however long the celebrations last, and afterwards they can be carefully packed away and stored until the next occasion arises.

The core material used, the hidden thread around which the garland is composed, will depend on the weight and volume of the decorative materials. You can use tightly coiled paper ribbon, florists' silver wire or thicker gauges, fine twine, string, cord, or rope. Just as for fresh-flower garlands, you may choose to conceal the core beneath a wrapping of dry hay or sphagnum moss, or bind on a foundation of readily-available (and in this case dried or preserved) foliage.

To outline the edge of the wedding cake table or the top table at the reception, you might compose a summery-looking garland on a core of unfurled paper ribbon, in a colour that matches or complements the overall scheme chosen by the bride. If you were given enough advance notice, you might even have the opportunity to dye some plant materials, such as sea lavender or gypsophila, especially for the occasion.

Small posy baskets of dried
rosebuds, lavender, and
gypsophila – pretty decorations
for a dressing table – would
make thoughtful gifts for
friends of all generations.
Opposite

WIRING DRIED FLOWERS

1 To bind a flower which has a reasonable length of stem, such as the air-dried rose and the delphinium shown here, place a stub wire close against the stem and bind the two together with silver wire.

You Will Need

stub wires ● roll of florists' silver wire ● wire cutters ● florists' scissors ● gutta percha (floral) tape ● scissors

2 To cover the false wire stem, wrap one end of a length of gutta percha (floral) tape around both the rose stem and the wire. Holding the wire in one hand and the tape in the other, twist the flower so that the tape is wrapped around the wire. Each twist of the tape should overlap and stick to the previous one. Fasten off the tape just before the end of the wire.

3 To wire dried flowers which have very short stems, such as the ranunculus shown here, which was dried in silica gel crystals, place a stub wire close against the short stem length and bind them together with silver wire. Bind the false wire stem with gutta percha (floral tape) as described.

4 To wire a flower which has no stem – strawflowers are a frequent example – push a stub wire through the flower from the base. Bend a short hook in the top of the wire and pull it down so that the hook is concealed within the flower centre. Bind the false wire stem with gutta percha (floral) tape .

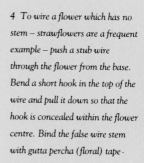

For a decoration on a larger scale, to drape across a church or barn door at a harvest festival or Thanksgiving, you could wrap a length of rope with hay (green twine is a suitable binding material) and tie on bunches of oats, wheat, dried vine leaves, and dahlias. If you use several strands of raffia or twist them into slender plaits finished with straggly bows, the ties can form an attractive part of the overall design.

As the 'Midsummer Hay Ring' illustrates, the hay can be revealed to decorative advantage, and it is not necessary to cover it completely with the decorative materials. This ring, which could convey the brightest of welcomes to guests arriving for a barbecue or garden party, is composed on a double copper-wire ring form, available from florists. The flowers are formed into bunches, bound with silver wire, and attached to the ring with staples made from bent stub wires.

Wire ring forms, which are more useful than decorative, do need concealing. You can do this in a number of ways to create floral rings for a variety of moods. Bind the ring with natural or coloured raffia, and attach dried herbs like fennel, marjoram, bay and sage, bunches of dried chillies, and heads of garlic for a practical kitchen decoration. Or bind the ring with paper ribbon, attach dried-flower posies or individual flower heads, and finish the design with a flourish with a large paper bow. It's a delightful notion for a nursery or young girl's room.

Vine wreath forms and those made of twisted willow or grass stems, all available from florists, have natural credentials, and may be fully or partly covered with decorative materials. You can attach bunches of lavender and a cluster of strawflowers to a trio of bleached willow rings, a minimal but aromatic decoration suitable for a bathroom, or cover a vine wreath with overlapping lavender bunches and dried-flower posies until the base is no more than a hidden asset.

Dry foam rings, available in sizes from 15cm (6in) to 30cm (12in) in diameter, call for a different technique. Here is a chance to use dried flowers, seedheads, and leaves on the shortest of stems, or, if you use clear, quick-setting adhesive or hot glue, ones with no stem at all. To make a thoughtful christening gift you could cover a ring with snippings of sea lavender and tansy, goldenrod and delphinium, love-in-a-mist and marjoram, and arrange a few rosebuds at intervals. Or, for a harvest decoration, outline a ring with short sprays of oats, and pack it with colourful strawflowers and seedheads to display on a door or wall, or to edge a rugged basket.

POTPOURRI

In days gone by large country households employed a mistress of the potpourri, who had the enviable task of composing aromatic blends of dried petals, leaves, spices, and oils, some displayed in decorative bowls and others sewn into fine linen, to scent the rooms and mask unwelcome odours. Today, although we no longer have this underlying need for potpourri, the therapeutic joy of composing an individual perfume from flowers gathered in the garden or saved from a gift bouquet is as compelling as ever.

There are two basic types of potpourri, one made by the 'moist' and the other by the 'dry' method. In the past, rose petals were at the heart of both, since Provence and cabbage roses grew in abundance in Elizabethan gardens, and their petals held their fragrance for many months. Today, as potpourri grows in popularity, the dry type may be made from any blend of dried materials, chosen as

Celebrate the harvest with a ring of oats, strawflowers, rosebuds, and love-in-a-mist seedheads. It could be used to add personality to a collection of baskets, hung on a door or a wall, or propped up as the centre-piece of a buffet table. **Above**

much for their colour and texture as for their odour. Any lack in this latter quality can be compensated for by the addition of more essential oils and spices.

THE MOIST METHOD

Traditional moist potpourri is made with rose petals dried in the sun (or oven) until they are leathery, but not crisp. The petals are packed into a moisture-proof box (not a tin) between layers of coarse salt – three cups of petals to one of salt – and are covered with a lid and set aside for ten days. During this time the salt will draw out the remaining moisture from the petals, and the mixture will first ferment and then form a block. Now the creative part of the process begins. Break up the block into a jar or crock, stir in 45g (3tbsp) of a mixture of ground spices such as allspice, cinnamon, cloves, mace, and nutmeg, and 45g (3tbsp) ground orris-root powder as a fixative, which you can buy in healthfood stores.

Cover the container and set it aside, except for a daily stir, for six weeks, then stir in two or three drops of an essential plant oil such as rose oil (attar of roses), rose geranium, or bergamot oil. Cover and store for a further two weeks before using. For visual variety, you can substitute marigold, larkspur, carnation, peony, or other petals for a proportion of the rose petals, or stir in a few rosebuds or chamomile flowers when you add the oils.

THE DRY METHOD

The dry method of making potpourri uses, as the term indicates, fully-dried petals, flowers, herbs, and leaves. These and other plant materials, such as tiny cones, wood shavings, and whole spices, are mixed with ground spices, orris-root, and essential oils, covered and then stirred once a day for six weeks. There are no hard and fast rules about quantities and proportions, but an allowance of 30–45g (2–3 tbsp) ground spices, 30g (2tbsp) ground orris-root powder, 10g (2tsp) dried lemon, orange, or lime peel, and two drops essential oil to every four cups of dried plant material makes a pleasantly balanced mixture.

Exactly how you dry the plant material is a matter of choice. The traditional method involves spreading out the petals, flowers, and leaves on a woven tray, and leaving it in a shady spot in the garden to dry in the heat of the sun. Instead, you can take as examples a handful of sweet-scented lily-of-the-valley flowers picked from the stalks or lemon verbena leaves, spread them in a single layer on a baking tray, and dry them for two or three days in a warm cupboard, or about half an hour in an oven at the lowest temperature and with the door slightly ajar. Or you can spread the materials on a microwave-safe plate or dish and dry them in a microwave at low power for about 10–12 minutes. Stir the materials from the sides of the tray inwards every couple of minutes, remove when crisp

A variety of floral ring decorations composed on vine wreath forms, dry foam rings, and twisted willow rings. They can harmonize with any room scheme using inexpensive materials like grasses, oats, and other seedheads, through honesty, strawflowers, and statice to more precious materials such as dried rosebuds and delphinium. **Opposite**

Potpourri, which is both an environmental perfume and a design accessory, can be displayed in open bowls, baskets or, as here, in stylish ornaments. **Left**

POTPOURRI RECIPES

Cottage Garden mix
(dry method)

1 cup dried lavender flowers
1 cup dried rose petals
1 cup dried pinks (*Dianthus*)
1 cup dried scented geranium leaves
15g (1tbsp) ground cinnamon
10g (2tsp) ground allspice
5g (1tsp) dried grated lemon peel
30g (2tbsp) dried orris-root powder
2 drops rose oil
Mix ingredients together in a covered container, and set aside for six weeks. Stir daily to distribute the fragrances.

Woodland mix
(dry method)

1 cup dried lime seedpods, or 'keys'
1 cup cedar bark shavings
1 cup sandalwood shavings
1 cup small cones
15g (1tbsp) whole cloves
15g (1tbsp) star anise
1 stick cinnamon, crushed
30g (2tbsp) dried orris-root powder
3 drops sandalwood oil
Mix ingredients together in a covered container and set aside for six weeks. Stir the contents daily to distribute the spices evenly.

Wedding bouquet mix
(dry method)

1 cup dried lily-of-the-valley flowers
1 cup dried white fuchsia flowers
1 cup dried white miniature roses
1 cup dried lavender leaves, crumbled
45g (3tbsp) dried orris-root powder
4 drops neroli (orange blossom oil)
4 drops lily-of-the-valley oil
This recipe does not use ground spices, as they would colour the white blossoms. Mix ingredients together in a lidded container. Stir every day for six weeks.

and papery, and allow to dry completely before putting into a lidded container.

You can store dried materials from one season to the next, ready to compose unseasonal and year-round potpourri blends, or use dried flowers and leaves from your plant collection. A single stem of air-dried larkspur, for example, can yield a wealth of bright blue florets, a bunch of deep pink cornflowers can add a colourful spark to a rose-petal mixture, and sprigs of air-dried purple sage add pungency to a potpourri garden blend of lavender, pinks, and carnations.

USING POTPOURRI

If your potpourri loses a little of its aroma over a period of time, it can be revived. Simply stir in another two or three drops of essential oil. And if the mixture loses its colour sharpness – as it will if set out in an open bowl in sunlight – just stir in a few dried miniature rosebuds, santolina flowers, tansy clusters, and the like.

Potpourri presents a delightful range of display options: open bowls to be stirred with the fingers to release the blended aromas; perforated 'pomander' bowls, porcelain or woven baskets – especially attractive with woodland mixtures of cones, bark, and sandalwood shavings; and cotton bags, sachets, and pillows to scent wardrobes and linen cupboards. An effective display can be made by filling a glass container with carnation and rose petal potpourri and placing it next to a profusion of dried garden flowers. Or cover a dry foam ring with glue and press on a golden potpourri blend of, say, forsythia and fuchsia flowers, marigold petals, and crushed lemon balm leaves. Both are romantic and pretty notions that demonstrate the versatility of petal power.

PRESSED FLOWERCRAFT

Pressing flowers and leaves between sheets of absorbent paper brings back memories of childhood, of sitting in a field and arranging buttercups and frondy grasses in heavy books. The key elements to success in this single-plane method of preserving are adequate moisture absorption, which is best provided by blotting paper, though smooth-surfaced kitchen paper and tissues are also suitable; a heavy weight or pressure, which can be achieved by pressing materials between pages in a large book, or in a flower press; a warm, dry atmosphere; and patience.

To be sure your pressed materials retain their original colours, it is important to change the absorbent papers

The traditional way to press flowers and leaves – between sheets of absorbent paper in a heavy book. The photograph shows (top to bottom) phlox flowers, carnation petals, alkanet (anchusa) flowers, and herb Robert stems. **Left**

two or three times during the first few days (and dry them for reuse). Then set the pressing medium aside and leave undisturbed for at least six months.

Deciding where to start, and which flowers, leaves, and grasses to press, can be one of the most delightfully overwhelming of all flowercraft choices. Wandering around a garden, snipping flowers, leaves, and even weeds from borders and flowerbeds can yield enough material to compose a pressed-flower posy, recreate a garden scene, or arrange an abstract design for months to come. You can gather materials from the countryside (though be sure they are not protected plants), give them a reviving drink when you get home, and press them for posterity. Or preserve flowers, petals, and foliage from a bunch bought from a market stall or – more nostalgically – a treasured gift bouquet.

It may seem like stating the obvious, but success relies on every part of the plant material coming into contact with the drying medium – the blotting paper. For this reason, it is essential to press materials of equal thickness on a single page. For this reason, too, thick-centred flowers, such as spray chrysanthemums, give disappointing results when pressed whole; the petals that do not make regular contact with the paper are likely to discolour and wither.

The trick with all such flowers – marigolds, gerberas, carnations, zinnias, roses, and many others – is to pull off each petal and press it separately. A single flower will then yield a multitude of petals, which can be reassembled more sparingly to create an image of the original. Trumpet-shaped flowers such as daffodils, freesias, and Peruvian lilies may be sliced in half vertically, using the sharp blade of a craft knife, and each half pressed separately, providing two for the price of one. Flat flowers such as pansies, primulas, borage, daisies, and hydrangea florets should be snipped off just below the calyces, and the pretty heads of umbellifers such as sheep's parsley

POTPOURRI INGREDIENTS

1 A handful of rose and carnation petals on a woven tray is set to dry by the most natural process of all – in the heat of the sun. Avoid placing petals in the full glare of the sun; a warm but shady place is best. Petals should be brought in before evening, when the dew would spoil them.

2 Ingredients which can be used to make potpourri. From the left, dried rosemary, lavender, and bay leaves, dried ground orris-root powder, dried rosemary leaves, a selection of essential oils, ground cinnamon, dried chillies and cinnamon sticks, whole cloves, a blend of dried flowers, and limes and lemons. The dried peel of citrus fruit is finely grated or chopped for use in the spice mixture.

Pressing flower petals as you gather them adds to the pleasure of the craft. The flower press is arranged with a pattern of sweet pea flowers, spray chrysanthemum petals, and ranunculus petals. **Left**

Pressed pansies, one of the most successful flowers to preserve in this way, were later arranged in a ring to create a Victorian-style decoration. Here, they are pressed between sheets of blotting paper in a flower press, and are shown with surgical tweezers for handling. **Opposite**

(Queen Anne's lace) and wild carrot may be pressed whole or as separate clusters, when they look like snowflakes. Short sprays of delicate flowers like forget-me-not, speedwell, and lady's mantle give variety to future designs. With this ultimate goal in mind, it is a good idea to press some buds, such as buttercups and daisies, and naturally curving stalks, such as those of clematis and, again, buttercup.

Pressed foliage is as essential to many representational compositions as it is to arrangements of fresh and dried flowers, and it is useful to have a selection of leaves chosen as much for their shape as for their colour. Clover, sheep's parsley, and aquilegia (columbine), with their delicate shapes; feathery fennel and cosmos; slender wallflower, willow, and lavender; heart-shaped geranium and ivy; and fallen leaves in all their shape and colour variety – there is so much design potential to press and store for future use.

Once flowers and leaves have been pressed, they will, like all dried materials, be brittle and damage-prone. Handle them carefully with plastic tweezers or surgical tweezers, and keep them in a warm, dry environment, in transparent packets. Use a small paintbrush (preferably) camel-hair) to position them in the design, and fasten in place with an opaque glue applied sparingly at intervals with the tip of a wooden cocktail stick. Cover each flower after gluing with a piece of clean white paper, and gently press it in place. When you are overlapping petals, flowers, and leaves, allow the glue of one layer to dry before imposing the next. When you have to leave the work overnight or when it has been completed, cover with a sheet of paper and then glass or a board weighed down with a heavy object to keep it flat.

Pressed-flower designs can be as simple or as creative and involved as you please. You can compose a small spray of flowers and leaves to make a gift tag or a greetings card; an alphabetical sampler to commemorate a baby's birth; a gentle curve of primulas, heather, and fern to complement an oval frame; or build up a realistic flower design using pressed grasses to represent a basket with flowers, buds, leaves, and stalks cascading in country-style profusion. Why not turn back the clock and create a cardboard ring of pressed pansies in the Victorian tradition, or compose a hoop of pressed autumn leaves and dried seedpods.

PRESSED FLOWERCRAFT EQUIPMENT

The makings of pressed-flower pictures, greetings cards, gift tags and labels: pressed flowers and leaves stored in transparent boxes and envelopes, children's craft glue and wooden cocktail sticks to apply it, surgical tweezers, a small paintbrush, scissors, a ruler, and iron-on transparent covering.

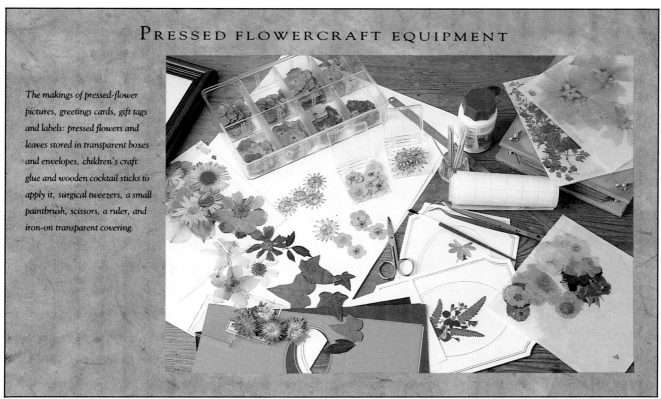

Whatever your choice of design may be, and whatever the end product you create, all pressed-flower compositions must be protected from dust and damage. Cover greetings cards and tags with film wrap, and pictures with glass or transparent iron-on mounts. To prevent colour fading, display all pressed-flower work away from strong light, especially direct sunlight.

DESIGNER FLOWERS

So far we have discussed ways of capturing the beauty of the flower garden in terms of drying, preserving, and pressing techniques – ways of holding plant materials in a state of decorative suspended animation. But alongside all the cultivated blooms in the florists' shops – and almost indistinguishable except at very close range – there is another colourful and long-lasting crop, that of 'designer' flowers. Often referred to as 'silk' flowers – although most are made of washable synthetic materials – artificial flowers crop up in all shapes and sizes. There is even a relatively new range that simulates dried flowers, of which the dried roses are especially convincing.

You can use designer flowers, which are mounted on stout wires, as you would dried ones, arranging them in dry stem-holding foam or anchoring them in a container fitted with crumpled wire mesh netting. If you find the wire stems are considerably longer than you need for your arrangement, just bend them back, to avoid shortening them permanently, and insert the double thickness of wire into the container.

Designer flowers make perfect partners for preserved materials. You can arrange a lavish-looking bunch of towering delphiniums and powder-blue hydrangeas with preserved copper-bronze beech leaves in a basket in the hearth; compose a meadow posy of cornflowers, poppies, and daisies with dried grasses to display in a sparkling glass or silver container on the dining table; or use scarlet designer poinsettias and carnations with fresh or preserved evergreens on a pedestal to decorate a church over the Christmas holidays.

You can display the made flowers in the steamiest of bathrooms and kitchens; a glass jug of white lilies would look stylish in the first instance, and a stone jar of narcissus and marigolds in the other. And for a lasting gift, you could arrange a basket of designer flowers, peonies, hydrangeas, roses, and statice. It would be a perfect token to celebrate a baby's birth or baptism, or to give to a friend who would especially appreciate the 'no watering needed' aspect of fabric flowers.

A pressed flower design in the Victorian tradition – a ring of pansies stuck in overlapping circles onto a piece of cardboard. The circlet would make a delightful decoration for a bedroom, whether it was mounted in an old frame, protected under a piece of glass on a table or dressing table, or covered with iron-on transparent plastic sheeting and hung on a wide ribbon over a bed. **Right**

Sometimes dinner- and teaware is just too pretty for mere eating and drinking! This posy-patterned milk jug is arranged with a selection of dried and dyed plant materials in a scheme reminiscent of old pink velvet. **Opposite**

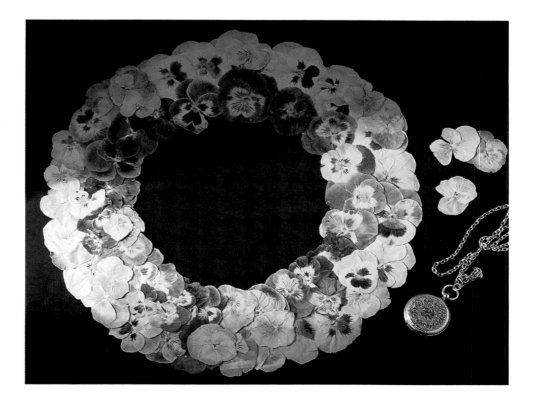

PRESERVING PLANT MATERIALS

The following table is a guide to some of the many plant materials you can preserve. It is not, and could not possibly be, a comprehensive list, but should help you select the appropriate method for any plant of your choice.

Plant material	Part of plant	Method
Acanthus	flower	air-drying
	leaf	glycerin
	seedhead	air-drying
Achillea (yarrow)	flower	air-drying
Anemone	flower	desiccant
Asparagus	leaf	microwave
Aspidistra (cast-iron plant)	leaf	glycerin
Astilbe (spiraea)	flower	air-drying
Bay	leaf	desiccant, glycerin
Beech	leaf	glycerin
Bell heather	flower	air-drying
Bells of Ireland	bract	air-drying, glycerin
Blackberry	leaf and berry	glycerin
Broom	short flower spray	desiccant
Bulrush	seedhead	air-drying
Buttercup	flower	desiccant
Camellia	flower	desiccant
Campion	flower	air-drying
Candytuft	flower	desiccant
	seedhead	air-drying
Caraway	seedhead	air-drying
Carnation	flower	desiccant
Celosia (cockscomb)	flower	air-drying
Chamomile	flower	air-drying, air-drying in water
Chestnut	leaf	glycerin
Chinese lantern (winter cherry)	seedhead	air-drying
Chive	flower	air-drying
Choisya	leaf	glycerin
Chrysanthemum	flower	desiccant
Clarkia	flower	air-drying
Clematis	leaf and seedhead	air-drying
Copper beech	leaf	air-drying, glycerin
Cornflower	flower	air-drying, air-drying in water, microwave
Corn cob (Indian corn)	seedhead	air-drying
Cow parsley (cow parsnip)	seedhead	air-drying
Daffodil	flower	desiccant
Dahlia	flower	desiccant
Daisy	flower	desiccant
Delphinium	flower	air-drying, desiccant
Dock	seedhead	air-drying
Dogwood	seedhead	air-drying
Dryandra	flower	air-drying
Elaeagnus (silver berry)	leaf	glycerin, microwave
Eryngium (sea holly)	flower	air-drying
Eucalyptus	leaf	glycerin
Fennel	leaf	air-drying, microwave
	seedhead	air-drying
Fern	leaf	glycerin
Fescue grass	seedhead	air-drying
Feverfew	flower	air-drying, air-drying in water, microwave
Fig	leaf	glycerin
Forsythia	short flower sprays	desiccant
Foxglove	flower	desiccant
Freesia	flower	desiccant
Gaillardia	seedhead	air-drying
Geranium	leaf, flower	desiccant
Giant hogweed	seedhead	air-drying
Globe amaranth	flower	air-drying
Globe artichoke	seedhead	air-drying
Goldenrod	flower	air-drying, microwave
Grape hyacinth	flower	desiccant
Gypsophila	flower	air-drying, air-drying in water, microwave
Hare's-tail grass	seedhead	air-drying
Heather	flower	air-drying
Holly	leaf	glycerin
Hollyhock	flower	desiccant
Honesty	seedhead	air-drying
Hop	leaf, bract	air-drying, glycerin
Hosta	leaf	glycerin
Hyacinth	flower	desiccant
Hydrangea	flower, bract	air-drying, air-drying in water, microwave

Ivy	leaf	glycerin
Japanese fatsia	leaf	glycerin
Jerusalem sage	flower, leaf, seedhead	air-drying
Knapweed	seedhead	air-drying
Laburnum	short flower sprays	desiccant
Lady's mantle	flower	air-drying, microwave
Larkspur	flower	air-drying, desiccant
Laurel	leaf	glycerin
Lavender	flower	air-drying, air-drying in water
	leaf	microwave
Lilac	small flower sprays	desiccant
Lily	flower	desiccant
Lily-of-the-valley	flower	desiccant
Linseed (flaxseed)	seedhead	air-drying
London pride (saxifrage)	flower	desiccant
Love-in-a-mist	flower, seedhead	air-drying
Love-lies-bleeding	seedhead	air-drying
Lupin (lupine)	flower	desiccant
	seedhead	air-drying
Magnolia	flower	desiccant
Mallow	flower	desiccant
	seedhead	air-drying
Maple	leaf	glycerin
Marguerite	flower	desiccant
Marjoram	flower	air-drying, microwave
Millet	seedhead	air-drying
Mimosa	flower sprays	desiccant, air-drying, air-drying in water
Mullein	seedhead	air-drying
Narcissus	flower	desiccant
Oak	leaf	glycerin
Oats	seedhead	air-drying
Old man's beard (*Clematis vitalba, C. virginiana*)	leaf, seedhead	air-drying
Onion	seedhead	air-drying
Orchid	flower	desiccant
Pampas grass	seedhead	air-drying
Pansy	flower	desiccant
Pearl (pearly) everlasting	flower	air-drying, air-drying in water
Peony	flower	air-drying, desiccant
Pine	cone	air-drying
Pink (button carnation)	flower	air-drying, desiccant
Polyanthus	flower	desiccant

Poppy	seedhead	air-drying
Pot marigold	flower	air-drying, desiccant
Primula (primrose)	flower	desiccant
Quaking grass	seedhead	air-drying
Ranunculus	flower	desiccant
Rhododendron	leaf	glycerin, microwave
Rose	bud, flower, leaf	air-drying
	fully-opened flower	desiccant
	hip	glycerin
Rosemary	leaf	glycerin, microwave
Rue	seedhead	air-drying
Sage	flower	air-drying
	leaf	air-drying, microwave
Santolina	leaf	air-drying, microwave
Sea lavender	flower	air-drying, air-drying in water
Sedge	seedhead	air-drying
Sedum (stonecrop)	flower	microwave
Senecio (groundsel)	leaf	air-drying, microwave
Silver-leaved everlasting	flower	air-drying
Sorrel	seedhead	air-drying
Statice	flower	air-drying
Stock	flower	desiccant
Strawflower	flower	air-drying
Sunflower	seedhead	air-drying
Sunray (swan river) everlasting	flower	air-drying
Sweet pea	flower	desiccant
Tansy	flower	air-drying, microwave
Teasel	seedhead	air-drying
Thistle	seedhead	air-drying
Timothy grass	seedhead	air-drying
Vine	leaf	desiccant
Wallflower	flower	desiccant
Wheat	seedhead	air-drying
Winged everlasting	flower	air-drying
Zinnia	flower	desiccant

BIRTHDAY BASKET

A 'posy' of dried flowers makes a thoughtful and long-lasting gift for a birthday, anniversary, or other celebration. It is a design with an illusory secret – which is revealed in the step-by-step photographs.

1 Choose a basket with a rugged texture, which contrasts well with the delicacy of the flowers and serves as an effective frame. The flowers range from deep pink through coral and pale mauve to dark blue.

2 Fix the plastic prong with a strip of clay, just off-centre in the base of the basket and press a piece of dry foam onto it. Cut short lengths of spiky flowers – blue larkspur, for example – and position to make a fan shape.

3 Complete the outline of larkspur, then fill in the shape with short stems of statice and rosebuds. Begin a row of strawflowers to give more visual weight close to the centre.

4 Cut short stems of three peonies – this design features two in deep pink with a central flower in pale pink. Place them close to the edge of the foam to help to conceal it.

5 Now comes the illusion. Cut the wheat stalks in a range of lengths so that some will extend just beyond the rim of the basket and others will fall somewhat shorter. Push the stalks into the foam so that they form a broad, thick fan shape.

6 Fill in the floral posy with sprigs of sea lavender to soften the outline and extend beyond the basket rim. Tie a bow with the ribbon, trim the ends at a slant and push the stub wire through the back of the loop. Bend the wire into a U-shape and press it into the foam between the peonies. Fill in any gaps with more sea lavender.

FLORAL TRIM

You Will Need

core material such as coiled paper ribbon, string, or cord ● roll of florists' silver wire ● selection of dried flowers such as statice, sea lavender, marjoram, delphinium, and strawflowers ● paper ribbon for bow ● pin, for fixing

A ribbon of dried flowers outlining the rim of a party table creates an air of festivity. You can compose the decoration in advance, confident that it will retain its crisp and colourful personality no matter how sultry the weather may be. And when the party's over you can pack the floral ribbon away until the next time.

1 A design of this kind, which is composed of short-stemmed posies, can be made up of clippings of dried flowers left over from other designs. It is a good idea to save all such materials in a box for this purpose. Here, coiled paper ribbon forms the core material, in a colour to tone with the flowers.

2 Make up small posies – varied or colour coordinated according to preference. Each posy in this design includes a strawflower to give it definition. Bind the stems with silver wire and cut to an even length.

3 Measure and cut the length of core required. Beginning close to one end of the core material, bind on the first posy with the flower heads towards the end of the coil. Bind on more posies, the heads of each one covering the stems of the one before.

4 When you have completed the
floral ribbon, pin it at intervals to
the tablecloth. Make one or two large
bows from the paper ribbon and pin to
the cloth.

5 A bird's-eye view of the decorated
table, the floral ring highlighted by
generous paper ribbon bows.

DESIGNER TREE

You Will Need

earthenware flower pot, about 12.5cm (5in) diameter ● plastic prong ● florists' adhesive clay ● modelling or self-hardening clay, or plaster of Paris ● straight but branched twig, such as apple wood ● 2 dry foam spheres, 7.5cm (3in) diameter ● secateurs (pruning shears) ● florists' scissors ● selection of dried flowers such as statice, sea lavender, broom bloom, rosebuds, cornflowers, and various everlastings ● 2.5cm-(1in-) wide checked ribbon ● a handful of dry sphagnum moss

Blossoming with strong primary colours set off by crisp white, this indoor tree makes a natural link between the garden and the home, and looks equally good in a doorway, on a windowsill, or a table.

1 The flowerpot may be painted with white emulsion to give the design a lighter, less earthy look. Select a ribbon that combines the colours of the flowers. Red, white, and blue gingham looks fresh and crisp.

2 Press a strip of adhesive clay onto the base of the plastic prong, fix it in the base of the pot and push a ball of modelling or self-hardening clay firmly onto it. Insert the twig and press the clay around it to hold it in place. Push the dry foam spheres onto the twig.

3 Cut short the flower stems – the shorter they are, the fewer you will need to cover the spheres and conceal the foam. Cover the first sphere with flowers in alternating colours, such as blue and white. Fill any remaining gaps.

4 Cover the second sphere in a similar way, using short stems of statice close to the foam and longer, wispy materials to provide a softer outline. Position a few rosebuds or other feature flowers at intervals among the statice. Tie a ribbon bow just below the higher sphere.

5 Tie more ribbons close to the pot, to trail over the rim. Instead of a multi-coloured check design, narrow ribbon or tape in each of the three principal flower colours may be used. Cover the holding material in the pot with dry moss.

RED, BRIGHT AND BLUE

A bundle of sun-bleached hogweed stems with their deep vertical ridges makes a highly textured holder for a colourful bunch of dried roses and larkspur. The stems were arranged in a rotund glass goldfish bowl, but they could be tied with raffia or paper ribbon and displayed, free-standing, as natural stem vases.

1 Bleached to a pale silver-grey, the hogweed stems make a dramatic foil for dried flowers in a vibrant colour range. Other suitable hollow stems, many of which may be found in the wild, are cow parsley (cow parsnip), wild parsnip, and hollyhock.

2 The sharp blade of a craft knife is best to cut the stems without splitting or tearing them. Cut them to more or less equal lengths so that they will extend a little above the rim of the container. Any side shoots on the stems will add interest to the composition. Gather the stems into a bundle, lower them into the container and twist so they have a circular slant.

3 Using each hogweed stem as a separate holder, position a row of larkspur stems, of uneven lengths, at the back of the design. Partly cover them with touches of fiery red. Dyed materials work well in this context.

4 Add some bottle brush stems, and then the foreground material – the dried roses complete with their leaves, and dark red strawflowers.

5 Unfurl a length of printed paper ribbon from both ends. Wrap the tightly-coiled centre section twice around the neck of the bowl and neaten the ends by cutting at a slant.

CANDLE GLOW

You Will Need

shallow bowl or dish • plastic prong • florists' adhesive clay • dry stem-holding foam • 2 plastic candle spikes • 2 candles of unequal length • selection of dried flowers and foliage (see above) • florists' scissors

Fully-opened roses and dense, petally carnations; exotic Singapore orchids and creamy madonna lilies; dainty spray carnations and deep purple anemones; sprays of fluffy mimosa and two-coloured elaeagnus – all the flowers and foliage in this cottage-style candle arrangement were dried in silica gel crystals in a microwave.

1 A shallow bowl on a short foot, lifting it just above the table top, helps to emphasize the inverted curve shape of the design. Choose candles in a neutral shade, or one that will not overshadow the delicate creamy tints of some of the flowers.

2 Press a short strip of florists' adhesive clay onto the base of the plastic prong, press it into the centre of the dish and push the foam block onto it. Push the candle spikes into the foam, one at each end. Tapering to a narrow point, these spikes do not break up the foam as a candle may do.

3 Position the candles in the two plastic holders and build up the design around them. Select sprays of a curving plant material such as dried broom and position with a few mimosa sprays to outline a deep, upward curve. Cover the holders on both sides with short sprays of dried variegated leaves.

4 Follow the outline of the foliage with slender flower sprays such as purple and cream Singapore orchids. Place larger, more rounded dried flowers such as carnations and roses close to the foam on all sides. Fill in the gaps with more roses and rosebuds.

5 Complete the design by grouping deep-coloured flowers in a cluster at the centre, and arranging small flowers such as spray carnations in threes and fours for maximum impact. Check that there are no flowers or leaves too close to the candle flames.

MIDSUMMER HAY RING

You Will Need

double ring copper-wire frame; the one used here is 25cm (10in) diameter ● bundle of dry hay, or dry sphagnum moss ● green binding twine ● roll of florists' silver wire ● stub wires ● wire cutters ● florists' scissors ● scissors ● selection of dried flowers such as sea lavender, statice, cornflowers, strawflowers, and carthamus 1.5cm- (½in-) wide ribbons in toning colours

Celebrate the height of summer with a dried flower hay ring composed of all the bright and beautiful colours of the rainbow. It can be hung as a brilliant party welcome on a gate, or an outside wall, or use it as a table decoration that will have guests reaching for their sunglasses.

1 A 'dished' type of copper-wire ring, which has the inner circle slightly lower than the outer one, is better for a design of this type, as it is easier to bind a deep layer of hay or moss. Choose ribbons that match the flowers as closely as possible for a fully coordinated look.

2 Tie the twine to the outer circle of the ring. Place handfuls of hay or moss over the ring and bind it on securely, taking the twine over and through the ring and pulling it tightly, to conceal it in the covering material. When the ring is completely covered, cut the twine and tie it to the ring.

3 Gather the flowers into small mixed posies, mixing the colours for the brightest effect. Cut the stems short and bind them with silver roll wire. Make several posies in this way.

4 Cut several stub wires in half and bend them to make U-shaped staples. Place a posy over the hay-covered ring, loop a staple over the stems and press into the hay. Bend back the wire ends and twist them around the back of the wire ring to secure.

5 Continue fixing more posies
around the ring so that the heads
of each one cover the stems of the one
before. Alternate the colours for the
brightest effect – the more blue
cornflowers and orange strawflowers
the merrier.

6 The ring may be completely
covered with posies, or a section of
the meadow hay may be left uncovered
as a textured feature. Fold the ribbon
lengths in half, twist half a stub wire
around the centre and press the ends
into the ring.

ALL BUNCHED UP

You Will Need

a selection of dried flowers such as larkspur, lady's mantle, marjoram, sea lavender, strawflowers, rosebuds, and hydrangea ● dried grasses ● roll of florists' silver wire ● florists' scissors ● patterned paper ribbon ● scissors

A hanging bunch of dried flowers, the interior design version of a posy, makes a charming wall decoration for any room in the home. This design was created for a young girl's bedroom, where it is displayed with a collection of Greek pottery.

1 Make your selection of dried flowers in colours that will blend perfectly with the proposed site for the decoration. Those to be placed at the back of the bunch will need suitably long stems.

2 Compose the dried flower bunch flat on a table. Place the longest stems, in this case the grasses, so that they will fan out at the back of the arrangement. Cover them with blue larkspur, the tips widely spaced and the stems close together.

3 Arrange stems of pink larkspur over the blue ones. Position a few marjoram stems in the centre and shorter sprays of lady's mantle from side to side. Arrange a few pink roses in the centre, and then strawflowers at varying heights. Place short stems of sea lavender so they will fan out at the sides of the bunch.

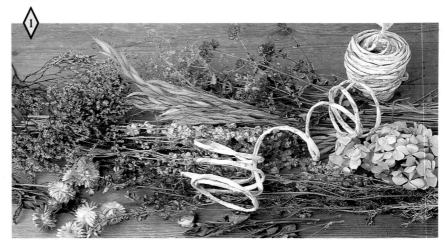

4 Bind the stems with silver wire. Before pulling the wire tight, rearrange the stems until the shape is pleasing. Tuck in a few short stems of hydrangea.

5 Unfurl the length of paper ribbon from each end but leave the centre section tightly furled. Wrap the centre section tightly around the stems and tie in a knot. Tie the ends into a bow, adjusting to make a full, rounded shape, and cut the ends at a slant.

COUNTRY GARDEN

Gather together the vibrant colours and myriad shapes of a herbaceous border in an arrangement that ensures the beauty of summer lingers on in your home. This design combines dried flowers with leaves and bracts preserved in glycerin.

1 The materials were preserved by several methods. The peonies, strawflowers, carthamus, and poppy seedheads were air-dried by hanging in bunches. In this way the peonies retain their long natural stalks and leaves, which can form a feature of the design. The sprays of variegated leaves were dried in silica gel crystals in a microwave and the leaves and bracts were preserved in a solution of glycerin and hot water.

2 Press the foam-holding container onto the blocks of dry foam until it leaves an imprint. Withdraw the container and cut around the foam. Cut strips of adhesive clay and press them onto the underside of the foam-holding container. Press this onto the neck of the vase and place the shaped foam in the dish. Arrange short sprays of variegated leaves low all around the foam. Position three long stems of bells of Ireland to define the centre height, and add sprays of eucalyptus.

3 Arrange the peonies to give a rounded shape. Where stems have to be shortened and leaves cut off, use these sprays to alternate with the flowers. Position short stems of eucalyptus around the base.

4 Arrange short stems of orange carthamus around the base of the design. Turn the vase around and arrange sprays of leaves and carthamus around the sides and at the back so that there will be no trace of the foam or its container.

5 Complete the design by arranging taller stems of carthamus between the peonies. Add two or three large poppy seedheads at one side and smaller ones, well recessed, at the heart of the design. Lastly, position a few bright orange strawflowers to reinforce the warm orange tones of the carthamus.

DUTCH INFLUENCE

Inspired by the magnificent paintings of the Dutch Masters, this arrangement is composed in a painted and gilded wooden urn. A cluster of fruits – pineapple, grapes, and pomegranates – and a jug of rich ruby wine complete the luxurious quality of the still-life group.

1 Choose a container with an interesting texture or colour combination, or paint one to harmonize with the room scheme and the flowers. Choose some long-stemmed flowers such as larkspur and air-dried roses to give the design height. If the flowers have been dried in the microwave, and have short stems, mount them on stub wires and bind with gutta percha (floral) tape.

2 Crumple the wire mesh netting and place it in the neck of the vase. Tuck in any stray ends. Cut short lengths of adhesive tape, twist them around the wire at intervals, and stick them to the rim of the container. When the design has been completed, the tape will be covered by the shortest of the flowers. Position the larkspur stems to create a fan shape.

3 Build up one side of the design. Arrange the roses – here they are deep and pale pink and rich cream – among the larkspur stems. Cut the stems in graduated lengths, so that some roses are positioned close to the rim of the container.

4 Build up the other side in a similar way, positioning full, rounded flowers such as roses, carnations, and clusters of hydrangea close to the base. This gives visual weight to the design. Add sprays of dried foliage for a variety of texture, and to give the arrangement a natural look.

5 Complete the arrangement by filling in all the gaps with more and more dried flowers until it has a generous and opulent appearance. You may like to mount groups of hydrangea bracts on stub wires and use these for contrasting highlights.

BRIDAL BOUQUET

You Will Need

roll of florists' silver wire • stub wires • wire cutters • white gutta percha (floral) tape • selection of dried flowers such as sea lavender, gypsophila, Singapore orchids, roses, rosebuds, lady's mantle, statice, hydrangea, and strawflowers • dried leaves such as pampas and broom sprays • 4cm- (1½in-) wide satin ribbon in two toning colours • scissors

The romance of roses, the veil-like quality of gypsophila, the luxury of Singapore orchids – they are all gathered together in a bouquet that could be carried by the bride or her attendants and would remain as a memento of the happy day.

1 Make a selection of flowers that complement the bridal scheme. Here the colours range from the pastel mauve of the sea lavender and statice to the deep purple of the Singapore orchids, hues which are enhanced by soft cream, white, and pale green.

2 Cut short sprays of sea lavender. Place a stub wire close against the stems and bind with silver roll wire. Bind the stems and false wire stem with a length of gutta percha (floral) tape, overlapping each twist as you do so. Bind clusters of hydrangea bracts, gypsophila, and short-stemmed roses in a similar way.

3 Gather together several flower sprays and foliage stems and arrange them in one hand so that they cascade in a natural, easy way. Rearrange until the combination is pleasing, then bind the group of false stems together with silver roll wire.

4 Add more wired and bound stems to the group, a few at a time, rearranging them until they make a pleasing shape. Alternate the full, round shapes of roses and strawflowers with wispy sprays of gypsophila and lady's mantle. Bind the bunch of false stems with ribbon, overlapping each twist all the way down.

5 Tie more ribbons around the handle to create generous bows with long, trailing ends. Neaten the ribbon ends by cutting them at a slant or into V-shapes. To avoid crushing the delicate flowers, place the bouquet in a deep vase or other container until the wedding day. To preserve it afterwards, keep well away from strong light.

BABY'S BOUQUET

The birth or baptism of a baby can be celebrated with a long-lasting floral gift. This design, which would be a delightful decoration for a nursery, is composed of a blend of dried flowers – sea lavender in two colours – and designer blooms in an open-work basket.

1 Select designer flowers as you would fresh ones, in colours that tone or harmonize and in a variety of shapes. Here, life-like hydrangeas were chosen to hold the centre of the design, with deep pink peonies, roses in a paler tint, and sprays of statice as a filler.

2 In an arrangement such as this, an open-work basket will reveal the stem-holding materials aiding the composition of the design. In an arrangement of all natural materials, lavender or thyme stems, or even sea lavender, could be woven in and out of the slats. As this basket may take pride of place among the nursery decorations, a toning pink paper ribbon was chosen instead. Unfurl the paper and thread it in and out, over and under each slat. Overlap the two ends at the back until the weaving is secure.

3 Cut two lengths of adhesive clay, press onto the underside of the prongs and press the prongs onto the base of the basket, one each side of the centre. Press the foam onto the prongs. Arrange sprays of sea lavender all around the foam to make a foundation for the designer flowers. Bend or cut the stem of one of the hydrangeas and place it at the centre back to define the height of the design.

4 Arrange the other hydrangeas, the peonies, and roses to make a dome shape, with the deep and pale pinks alternating. Fill in the spaces with designer statice. It is a matter of choice whether the artificial flower stems are cut – which requires wire cutters and a strong wrist – or bent so they can be used full length in another design. It is a question of choice, too, whether most or all of the leaves are discarded; they are usually far less realistic than the made flowers.

5 Fill in any spaces with sprays of sea lavender, which reinforce the 'natural' look of the display. Unfurl about 75cm (30in) of the paper ribbon and tie a bow. Fix the bow to the front of the basket with a piece of adhesive clay or a stub wire.

LAVENDER BLUE

The heady scent of lavender makes it a perfect component for a ring to display in a bedroom, a bathroom, beside a window seat, or wherever there is a hint of romance. A smaller ring could hang inside a wardrobe or over a decorative coathanger.

1 For the posies which are to alternate with the lavender bunches, choose flowers in soft, complementary colours – blue, cream, and green are ideal. If a hot-glue gun is not available, the bunches and posies can be fixed to the wreath form with stub wires bent into U-shaped staples.

2 Gather eight or ten lavender stems into a bunch, cut short the stems and bind them with silver wire. Make mixed posies – there are six in this design – with other dried flowers, arranging the full, rounded flowers like roses and cornflowers in the centre and the wispy sprays at the sides. Bind the stems with roll wire.

3 Run a thin strip of hot glue along the stems of the first lavender bunch and press onto the wreath form, holding it in place for a second or so while the glue sets. Stick on more bunches, the heads of each successive one covering the stems of the one before. Continue around the ring, spacing the lavender and mixed posies as desired.

4 Cut the ribbon into six equal lengths. Tie each length into a bow and trim the ends. Cut the stub wires in half and bend them to make U-shaped staples. Press five ribbon bows into the inside of the wreath form and one on top. Glue on extra strawflower heads if there are any gaps or silver wires visible.

5 Adjust the ribbon bows so they hang neatly and evenly. Hang the wreath form on a wall, or place it on a table or linen chest.

SUMMER CASUAL

Decorated with peonies and tied with pink and white gingham ribbons, this is a hat for the young at heart. Wear it on a summer picnic, or for an informal lunch in the garden. The very young could even wear this stylish and pretty hat to a country wedding.

1 Cut a piece of thick wire long enough to encircle the hat brim, and bend a hook into each end to make it easier to slip on and off the hat. Choose a ribbon in colours that tone with the flowers.

2 Cut a length of ribbon long enough to cover the wire circle, allowing a little extra to turn under the wire. Turn under one end to neaten it, wrap the ribbon close to the hook on one end of the wire and bind it in place with silver roll wire. Ease the ribbon around the wire circle, turn in the other end and bind it close to the second hook. Gather the dried flowers into four posies, with a peony, a rosebud, and a poppy seedhead in each. Cut the stems short and bind them with silver roll wire. Bind the first posy onto the ribbon-covered wire circle.

3 Bind on the remaining three flower posies so the heads of each successive one cover and conceal the stems of the one before. The design will have the appearance of a continuous ribbon of flowers. When the decoration is in place, slip the ribbon band over the hat and fasten the two hooks.

4 Make a bow from more ribbon and leave trailing ends. Bend half a stub wire to make a U-shaped staple, push it through the loop at the back of the bow and push the ends through the hat. Bend them back so they are flat against the inside of the crown.

5 Perfect for any casual summer occasion – several flower-decked hatbands can be made in a range of colours to fit any plain straw hat.

PETAL POWER

This rectangular glass tank seemingly filled with fragrant pink
potpourri has hidden depths. A piece of dry stem-holding foam allows
a collection of dried cottage-garden flowers and herbs to be arranged
just as they grow, in delightful profusion.

1 Select a potpourri mixture that
blends well with the colours of the
dried flowers in the arrangement. This
design incorporates a pink and yellow
mixture of rose and carnation petals.
For the prettiest effect, include some
large flowers among the selection –
peonies and carnations in this
arrangement – to give definition to the
design and avoid a speckled look.

2 Cut two strips of adhesive clay,
press one onto the base of each of
the plastic prongs and press the prongs
into the container. Cut the block of
foam to fit into the container, leaving a
gap of about 1.5cm (½in) all around
and extending about 2.5cm (1in) above
the rim. Push the foam onto the spikes
of the plastic prongs, to keep it in
place. Spoon the potpourri into the
container to fill the gaps on all sides
and conceal all but the top of the foam.

3 Begin the arrangement by making
a fan shape of a sparse and light-
weight plant material – pale and dark
mauve marjoram flowers were used
here. Cut short some of the stems and
position them so that the flowers thrust
forward. It is important that the
arrangement has depth and dimension,
and does not present a flat plane with
the front of the container.

4 Arrange the rosebuds at intervals through the design to follow the outline of the marjoram. Position some of the largest of the dried flowers – carnations and peonies – low at the front, with some flower heads overlapping the container rim. Arrange a fan shape of statice extending to each side of the design, cutting short the stems to be positioned at the front.

5 Fill in the design with the fluffy green and yellow stems of the lady's mantle – the very essence of a cottage garden. Gather the cornflowers into bunches and position them – the brightest blooms in the arrangement – in clusters. Check that the rim of foam is completely hidden by the flowers placed at the sides of the arrangement. Turn the container around and complete the reverse of the design.

A BATHROOM COVER-UP

You Will Need

*glass-covered dish ● florists'
adhesive clay ● scissors ● plastic
prong ● cylinder of dry stem-holding
foam ● knife ● selection of dried
flowers such as statice, helichrysum,
lady's mantle, cornflowers, and
rosebuds ● florists' scissors*

A dried-flower arrangement may seem paradoxical in a hot and steamy bathroom – but not if it is under permanent protection. This design, a modern version of a Victorian flower dome, is created on the pine base of a cheese dish and covered with the clear glass lid.

1 Select dried flowers in sharply contrasting colours so they do not blend into an unidentifiable mass when covered with the glass dome or lid. Blue, white, and yellow statice; yellow helichrysum, lady's mantle, and rosebuds; and blue cornflowers were used in this design.

2 Press a small strip of adhesive clay to the base of the plastic prong and press it onto the centre of the base. Cut the foam to the size and shape required and press it onto the prong. Arrange a ring of white statice around the base, the stems placed horizontally in the foam. Make a dome shape with yellow rosebuds. Put on the glass cover to check that the stems are not too tall.

3 Arrange short stems of blue and yellow statice between the rosebuds and then, to soften the effect, add short sprays of helichrysum and lady's mantle.

4 Position cornflowers evenly throughout the design. Turn the base around and check that it is equally well covered from every angle.

5 Once the cover is in place the dried flowers are well protected from any steam. To make a complete seal, press a narrow strip of modelling clay such as Plasticine all around the rim of the base and scatter a few highly-absorbent silica gel crystals among the dried flowers. Then press the cover onto the clay to complete the seal.

EASTERN RICHES

You Will Need

deep, round earthenware container; a flowerpot or jug would be suitable
* *piece of florists' wire mesh netting*
* *narrow florists' adhesive tape*
* *scissors* • *florists' scissors*
* *secateurs (pruning shears)*
* *selection of dried flowers and seedheads such as shumag, caspia, nigella Orient, bottle brush, and amaranthus; pine and fir cones could also be included.*

Capture the spirit of the East with an arrangement of exotic dried flowers and seedheads in rich glowing reds, woody browns, and subtle greens. The rough earthenware container, a traditional yogurt pot, is the centre of a collection of pottery gathered on holiday travels.

1 Choose dried materials varied in both texture and colour, and include some types with the look of intricately carved wooden flowers. Some florists sell bags of assorted materials simply labelled 'exotics'. If these are available, some of the flowers and seedheads will have to be mounted on stub-wire stems.

2 Crumple the wire mesh netting to fit into the neck of the container. Criss-cross two strips of adhesive tape over the mound of wire netting and press the ends to the rim of the container. Begin the design by placing some of the tallest stems in a fan shape. Cut some of the stems so that the height is graduated.

3 Fill in the design with some of the more solid shapes, grouping them together in twos and threes to maximize their impact. Place some stems so they dip over the rim of the container.

4 Remember that red and green are colours that complement each other, and position some of the red feathery flowers to nestle among the flattering green materials.

5 Complete the design by positioning some of the cone-like seedheads to cover the container rim while others provide the contrast of full, round shapes.

BRIGHT PERSONALITY

You Will Need

brass or copper container; it could be a jug or kettle • *piece of plastic-covered wire mesh netting* • *narrow florists' adhesive tape* • *scissors* • *florists' scissors* • *secateurs (pruning shears)* • *selection of dried and dyed seedheads such as Chinese lanterns (winter cherry), globe thistle (echinops), poppy, and thistle* • *dried and preserved foliage*

An old brass watering-can, burnished until it shines, holds a riot of colourful materials. Some glow with their natural hues and others – the poppy seedheads, sprays of preserved and bleached leaves, and miniature thistles – have been dyed to coordinating shades. This is a perfect design for a sun-room or conservatory, fireplace, or porch.

1 Chinese lanterns (winter cherry), the most vibrant of all seed carriers, give this design its colour impact. The purple seedheads provide a muted but striking contrast, and the bleached and dyed foliage link the two elements. A few spiky green leaves, dried in the microwave, break the two-colour monopoly.

2 Crumple the wire netting and fit into the neck of the container. Anchor it with two or three short lengths of adhesive tape wrapped around a strand of wire and stuck onto the container rim. Arrange the foliage to make a fan shape with the tallest stems in the centre and the shortest ones at the side.

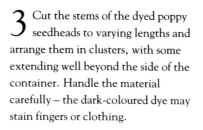

3 Cut the stems of the dyed poppy seedheads to varying lengths and arrange them in clusters, with some extending well beyond the side of the container. Handle the material carefully – the dark-coloured dye may stain fingers or clothing.

4 Arrange the smaller plant material
– the spiky dyed thistles – in tight
clusters, grouping short stems close
around the rim of the container, where
they will conceal the crumpled wire.

5 Repeat the fan shape of the
bleached leaves, poppy seedheads
and thistles on the other side of the
container, angling some stems almost
horizontally into the crumpled wire
mesh. Distribute stems of the orange
Chinese lanterns (winter cherry)
evenly through the design, with some
dipping low over the container, caught
in its reflection.

SCENTED RING

You Will Need

*stem ring; the one used here is
20cm (8in) diameter ● potpourri,
about 100g (4oz) ● hot glue
● dried flowers such as rosebuds
and sea lavender ● roll of florists'
silver wire ● half a stub wire
● 4cm- (1½in-) wide satin ribbon
● scissors*

A preformed ring covered with colourful and fragrant potpourri and decorated with a dried flower posy makes a romantic design for a bedroom, and a charming gift for family and friends of all ages.

1 You could use a dry foam ring in place of the stem ring, but it does not have the same aesthetic appeal in such a pretty decoration. Choose potpourri in colours to complement the chosen room scheme, or in the favourite colours of the recipient.

2 Hot glue gives the most quick and easy results, but a clear all-purpose glue may be used instead. Spurt the glue onto the ring a little at a time, and press the potpourri onto it. Take care not to burn your fingers when using hot glue. Allow to cool for a few seconds before pressing on the petals.

3 Work all around the ring, gluing and pressing on the petals until the form is covered on top, both inside and outside. If there are any gaps, spurt on a little more glue and add more petals. Glue some of the most colourful petals on top to give the ring a bright appearance.

4 Arrange the dried flowers to make a small posy. Cut short the stems and bind them with silver wire. Bend the stub wire in half to make a U-shape, loop it over the stems and press the ends of the wire into the ring, to secure the posy on top.

5 Tie the ribbon around the ring form, bringing the ends over the top, where they will cover the posy stems and binding wire. Tie the ribbon into a bow and trim the ends neatly.

Note
Place the ring away from strong light. If it fades and loses some of its fragrance, glue on a few more petals and sprinkle the decoration – but not the ribbon – with a few drops of potpourri oil, or an essential oil such as neroli.

WINTER GARDEN

You Will Need

shallow square or rectangular basket or box; the container used here is 20cm (8in) square ● dry stem-holding foam ● knife ● selection of dried materials such as wheat, carthamus, poppy seedheads, and thistles ● florists' scissors ● dried mushrooms ● stub wires ● wire cutters ● dry sphagnum moss

Think of a field of wheat at twilight; think of the dramatic shapes of seedheads as they dry in the flower borders; think of the excitement of coming across a patch of wild mushrooms in a meadow – and bring all those elements together in an unusual composition of contrasting plant materials.

1 This design features plant materials found in the wild, and others with dramatic rather than delicate shapes. To dry fungi, place on a rack in the oven for several hours at the lowest temperature, or leave for several days in a warm, dry place, such as an airing cupboard or boiler room.

2 Cut the foam block into pieces that will fit tightly into the container. The foam should come to within about 2cm (¾in) of the top of the basket. It is not necessary to use any holding or fixing materials. Cover the foam with moss so that it comes just above the basket rim.

3 Cut the stub wires in half and push a wire into the stalk of each of the dried mushrooms. Arrange the mushrooms in a group at one corner of the basket, some on short stalks overlapping the rim and others standing tall.

4 Press short-cut stalks of carthamus into the foam close to the mushrooms. Position poppy seedheads, their stalks cut to uneven lengths, in a group behind the fungi.

5 Add taller stems of the orange carthamus to form a group. Create a patch of wheat in the corner opposite the fungi, and position short stalks of dried thistle to add to the textural interest. Use stub wires to 'tease' the moss between the stalks and ensure that there are no tell-tale signs of stem-holding foam.

PRESSED INTO SERVICE

A ring of pressed autumn leaves and dried seed carriers makes an unusual and highly-textured wall decoration. To protect the plant materials, place them behind glass in a frame, mount them on coloured cardboard and cover with transparent film, or display them under the glass top of a coffee table.

1 Draw the inner and outer rims of the ring on the cardboard, and cut it out. This design is 28cm (11in) diameter. Make the selection of pressed leaves as varied as possible in both shape and colour.

2 Put small dabs of glue onto the tip, centre, and stem end of each leaf and arrange them, overlapping, so the tips extend beyond the inner and outer rims of the cardboard ring. Cover the leaves with a sheet of plain paper and press firmly with your hand. Put dabs of glue at intervals on the back of a large and shapely leaf, place this onto the first layer, and press it in place.

3 Continue to build up layers of leaves and seed carriers so that the design is full of interest and contrast.

4 The completed ring, an interpretation of a carpet of fallen leaves in a woodland, looks best mounted on colours in keeping with the autumnal theme. Choose muted greens, rich creams, clear greys, and burnt umber in preference to strong or primary colours which may overshadow the subtle colour blend of the leaves.

HALLOWEEN HIGHLIGHT

You Will Need

piece of twisted vinewood, driftwood, or other well-shaped branch • well-shaped, forked apple or other twigs, preferably covered with lichen • small quinces, or golden apples or pears • clear quick-setting glue or hot glue • stub wires • wire cutters • small waterproof dish • slice cut from a cylinder of absorbent stem-holding foam, soaked in water • flowers such as single spray chrysanthemums • pyracantha (firethorn) berries • foliage such as ivy and berberis (barberry) • florists' scissors • secateurs (pruning shears) • 2 apples • apple corer • 2 candles

Heighten the party atmosphere and brighten the buffet table with a forest of ideas for Halloween. This creation – which can be extended to any length desired – comprises a piece of gnarled and twisted wood, a bunch of apple twigs, and a small harvest of quinces. Add a handful of golden flowers, berries, and leaves and a couple of golden candlesticks, and you are all set to turn the lights down low.

1 To create the effect appropriate to Halloween, select the wood, twigs, and leaves with care. The more gnarled, twisted, forked, and green-encrusted the branches the better; the more purple and veined the ivy leaves, the more spooky the effect will be.

2 Begin by attaching the fruit to the twigs. You can do this in one of two ways, by gluing or wiring. If you decide to use glue, attach the fruits where the twigs fork and there is the largest area of contact. Cover the twig with glue or hot glue, press on the fruit and hold it in place for a few seconds until the glue sets.

3 If you prefer to wire on the fruits, push a stub wire through the back of each one, bring the two wire ends together and twist them firmly. Wrap the wire around a twig and twist the fruit until it rests neatly on the surface.

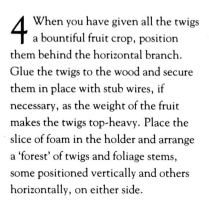

4 When you have given all the twigs a bountiful fruit crop, position them behind the horizontal branch. Glue the twigs to the wood and secure them in place with stub wires, if necessary, as the weight of the fruit makes the twigs top-heavy. Place the slice of foam in the holder and arrange a 'forest' of twigs and foliage stems, some positioned vertically and others horizontally, on either side.

5 Cut short sprays of the chrysanthemums and some separate flowers and arrange them in the foam. Add sprays of the autumn leaves – berberis (barberry) in this design – and more ivy leaves. The largest ones may be used to conceal the foam. Snip off any flowers that look too crowded or confusing.

6 Position the flower group at one end of the 'fallen branch' where it continues the line of the wood. Use an apple corer to scoop out the centre of the apples and insert a candle in each one. Keep lighted candles away from children or pets.

THANKSGIVING FESTIVAL

You Will Need

wide, shallow and sturdy basket
• waterproof liner such as a baking dish • absorbent stem-holding foam, soaked in water • narrow florists' adhesive tape • scissors • selection of flowers such as spray chrysanthemums, roses, hydrangeas, and sedum • selection of autumn foliage such as alder, ivy, blackberry, and old man's beard • selection of fruits and seedheads such as crab apples, blackberries, rosehips, and sloes • 3 pomegranates • stub wires • florists' scissors • secateurs (pruning shears)

A rustic basket filled with flowers, fruit, and foliage can take its place with pride at a harvest festival or at Thanksgiving, and looks equally good in the home, chapel, or church. Set in a window, shafts of golden autumn sunlight will flatter the russet colours of the plant materials, or use the composition to bring a warm glow to a shadowy corner.

1 The colour scheme of the arrangement makes the most of the tints and tones of the season, from the near-purple of the blackberry leaves and sedum to the pale pink of the climbing roses and hydrangeas; from the rosy blush of the pomegranates to the apricot hue of the spray chrysanthemums.

2 Place the waterproof liner in the basket. Place one whole block of foam in the dish and a half block in front of it. Secure each block in place by taping it from side to side with adhesive tape, over the foam and onto the container. Take another strip from front to back, over both of the foam blocks. Arrange some tall stems and branches at the back of the basket – fruiting crab apple looks magnificent – and short stems at the front on the other side.

3 Prepare the fruits that comprise the focal point of the arrangement. Pomegranates were used here but rosy apples, pears, or bunches of grapes could be used instead. Thread a stub wire through the fruit, close to the base. Twist the wire firmly and bend a hook in one end, to loop over the basket rim or into the foam.

4 Position the pomegranates or other fruit at the front of the arrangement, one dipping low over the basket rim, one resting on it, and the other close to the foam.

5 Cut the stems of the spray chrysanthemums to varying lengths and position them, tall, medium-height, and short, throughout the design.

6 Begin to fill in the arrangement with the thick, ruby-red heads of sedum, which make a striking contrast to the neighbouring chrysanthemums. Add accents of glossy red rosehips, and pale pink hydrangeas.

7 Position partly-opened roses next to the rosehips, and blackberry stems to border the design on one side. Complete the design by adding short sprays of glossy ivy; the green leaves make an interesting contrast to the autumn tints.

8 In this bountiful season, this fruit and flower arrangement looks at its best surrounded by more autumnal crops. A generous pile of apples and pears, marrows and pumpkins, and the pick of the falling leaves all add to the look of plenty.

GARLAND OF EVERGREENS

You Will Need

thick cord or rope ● *dry hay or sphagnum moss* ● *green binding twine* ● *scissors* ● *evergreens such as blue pine* ● *dried wheat* ● *florists' scissors* ● *secateurs (pruning shears)* ● *gold spray paint* ● *selection of pine and fir cones* ● *hot glue* ● *7.5cm- (3in-) wide decorative ribbon* ● *stub wire*

The custom of bringing evergreens into our homes has its origins in the ancient world, when people believed them to have magical powers. A garland of evergreens, whether it is composed of blue pine, holly, or ivy, has the power to transform a corner of a room, a fireplace, or an arch and make it a decorative focal point at Christmastime.

1 This simple garland is composed of blue pine. Other materials could include Norwegian pine – the lower branches cut from the Christmas tree, perhaps – juniper, cypress, or many other evergreen species.

2 Measure the area where the garland is to hang, allowing for gentle curves and drapes and cut the rope to the required length. Tie the twine at one end of the rope. Take handfuls of hay or moss, wrap the material around the rope and bind it by taking the twine around it. Continue until the length, or lengths of rope are completely concealed beneath the natural material.

3 Cut the evergreen in short lengths and sprays. Place the first one over the hay-covered rope and bind it in place with the twine. Bind on more sprays, each one covering the stem end of the one before.

4 Gather the wheat in bunches of about six or seven heads and cut the stems to a total length of about 17.5cm (7in). Bind the stems with green twine. Place the bunches of wheat well apart on a newspaper and spray the heads with gold paint. Turn them over and spray them on the other side. Leave the paint to dry. Bind bunches of gilded wheat with the evergreens along the garland, first on one side and then the other.

5 When the length of the garland is completed, attach the cones. Drizzle spots of hot glue onto the pine at intervals and press on a cone. For the best appearance, alternate cones with long and rounded shapes.

6 Hang the garland in position and adjust it so that the evergreens, and not the hay-covered rope, are forward looking. Tie the ribbon into a bow, neaten the ends by cutting them at a slant, and thread the stub wire through the loop at the back. Attach the bow to the garland.

CHRISTMAS CHEER

You Will Need

large flat plate; the one used here is 30cm (12in) diameter ● 2 plastic prongs ● florists' adhesive clay ● scissors ● absorbent stem-holding foam, soaked in water ● fruits, nuts, and berries such as pineapple, pomegranates, satsumas, lychees, pecans, and iris seeds ● flowers such as carnations, roses, and spray chrysanthemums ● evergreens such as ivy, yew, mahonia, eucalyptus, and cypress ● florists' scissors ● secateurs (pruning shears)

Rose-coloured fruits and glossy nuts; gilded evergreens and glowing berries; coral carnations and vibrant roses – the materials bring together the natural gifts of the season in this outstanding Christmas decoration to display on a sideboard or side table, or as the centre of attraction on a buffet table.

1 The deep coral shades of the pomegranate and the iris seeds provided the colour cue for this arrangement; the principal flowers – the carnations and roses – were chosen to fit in with the scheme.

2 Make sure the plate is absolutely dry. Cut two short strips of adhesive clay and press one onto the underside of each of the plastic prongs. Press these onto the plate, one just behind the central point and one in front of it and to the right. Push blocks of soaked foam onto the prongs. Begin the arrangement by positioning a selection of evergreens to outline the height on one side and the depth of the design on the other.

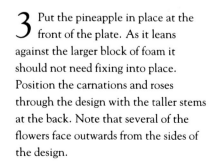

3 Put the pineapple in place at the front of the plate. As it leans against the larger block of foam it should not need fixing into place. Position the carnations and roses through the design with the taller stems at the back. Note that several of the flowers face outwards from the sides of the design.

4 Position stems of spray chrysanthemums behind the other flowers where they will be seen as fillers rather than feature flowers. Arrange the iris berries on tall, medium, and short stems to distribute their contrasting texture throughout the design. Arrange trails of ivy low at the front.

5 Using hot glue, or quick-setting clear glue, stick several lychees together in a deep cluster. Thread a stub wire through a gap between the fruits, position them close to the pineapple and push the wire into the foam. Glue a cluster of pecans and position in a similar way, on the opposite side. Thread a stub wire through the back of a satsuma, twist the two ends and push the wire into the foam above the cluster of lychees. Tuck

a pomegranate under the cascade of fruits and another (not illustrated) behind the iris stems on the other side.

6 Complete the design by adding more sprays of evergreens including, perhaps, trails of ivy sprayed with gold paint. Cover all traces of foam at the back of the arrangement with sprays of cypress and ivy. Arrange piles of fruit close to the design to complete the effect.

KISSING RING

A bundle of wispy evergreens, clusters of gilded seedheads, a few sprigs of mistletoe, and two glittering bows make this the prettiest yuletide wreath ever. Hang it as a sign of welcome on the front door, on an internal wall or door or – a romantic notion – over a bed.

1 The wreath is designed to have an informal and slightly wayward look, so it is a good idea to avoid the darkest and heaviest of evergreens. Here, short sprays – hedge clippings – of lime-green cypress, slender trails of small-leafed ivy, eucalyptus, and mistletoe were used.

2 Cover the work surface with newspaper or scrap paper and spread out the wheat and linseed (flaxseed) seedheads, the artificial flowers, and any evergreens to be sprayed with gold paint. The degree of gilding in the design is a matter of personal preference. Here, a few of the ivy and eucalyptus stems were spatter-sprayed, but the leaves were not covered completely. Spray the materials on one side, then turn over and spray on the other. Leave to dry.

3 Gather the wheat into bunches of four or five stalks and bind them with silver wire. Gather the linseed (flaxseed) into bunches of uneven lengths – this gives the wispy look to the finished outline which is a feature of the design. Cut the evergreens into short lengths.

4 Cut several stub wires in half and bend them over to make U-shaped staples. Place a bunch of evergreens over the stem ring, loop a 'staple' over the stalks and press the wire ends into the wreath base.

5 Take a bunch of wheat and a piece of mistletoe, place so the heads cover the evergreen stems and staple in place. Continue adding evergreens and the other materials all around the ring, the heads of one cluster or bunch covering the stalks of the previous one.

6 Position the sprayed artificial flowers around the ring in an asymmetrical way. Wire stems can be pushed horizontally through the evergreens and into the wreath base. Tie two bows with the ribbon and neaten the ends by cutting them at a slant. Push half a stub wire through the loop at the back of each bow and insert into the wreath form.

7 Hang the wreath where it will catch flattering shafts of light to emphasize the gilding. To give your Christmas decorations a coordinated look, you could compose a smaller version of the wreath for a table decoration.

CHRISTMAS GREETINGS

Welcome callers with a simple evergreen door posy, or make several to decorate the house during the festive season.

1 Cover the work surface with newspaper and spray a few heads of wheat and some trails of ivy with gold paint. Turn the materials over and spray them on the other side. Leave them to dry. Gather the wheat in a bunch of uneven lengths and bind the stems with silver wire. Tie the grass stems into a bunch and wire them.

2 Place the largest component, the blue pine, on the table and arrange the other materials over it. Rearrange them until they form a pleasing shape. Bind all the stems together with silver wire. Tie the ribbon around the stems, tie into a bow and trim the ends by cutting at a slant.

TARTAN TRIO

You Will Need

plain white candles; these are 30cm (12 in) long ● snippings of evergreens such as blue pine, cypress, holly, yew, and box ● artificial holly berries ● seedheads, sprayed with gold paint ● secateurs (pruning shears) ● roll of florists' silver wire ● florists' scissors ● 4cm- (1½ in-) wide and 2.5cm- (1in-) wide ribbons ● scissors

Give plain white candles a festive look with bright trimmings of evergreens, berries, and ribbons. You can use them to decorate a window, a mantelpiece, or the dining table.

1 Cut short lengths of mixed evergreens and seedheads. Place a few stems against a candle and bind in place with silver wire. Add more stems, and bind in place around the candle until it is decorated with a ring of evergreens. Secure the binding wire. Hook the wires of the berry decorations over the silver wire. Tie a ribbon around the candle to conceal the wire, tie it in a bow and trim the ends.

2 Display the candles among cuttings of evergreens. Do not leave lighted candles unattended.

INDEX